Anti-Movements
in America

IS AMERICA
SAFE FOR DEMOCRACY?

WILLIAM McDOUGALL

ARNO PRESS

A New York Times Company

New York / 1977

Editorial Supervision: JOSEPH CELLINI

———◆———

Reprint Edition 1977 by Arno Press Inc.

Reprinted from a copy in
  The University of Illinois Library

ANTI-MOVEMENTS IN AMERICA
ISBN for complete set: 0-405-09937-1
See last pages of this volume for titles.

Manufactured in the United States of America

———◆———

Library of Congress Cataloging in Publication Data

McDougall, William, 1871-1938.
    Is America safe for democracy?

    (Anti-movements in America)
    Reprint of the 1921 ed. published by Scribner,
New York.
    1. Race--Addresses, essays, lectures. 2. Civi-
lization--Addresses, essays, lectures. 3. United
States--Civilization--20th century--Addresses, essays,
lectures. 4. Eugenics--Addresses, essays, lectures.
I. Title. II. Series.
CB195.M3   1977   301.45'1'042   76-46088
ISBN 0-405-09961-4

IS AMERICA
SAFE FOR DEMOCRACY?

IS AMERICA
SAFE FOR DEMOCRACY?

SIX LECTURES GIVEN AT THE
LOWELL INSTITUTE OF BOSTON, UNDER THE TITLE
"ANTHROPOLOGY AND HISTORY, OR
THE INFLUENCE OF ANTHROPOLOGIC CONSTITUTION
ON THE DESTINIES OF NATIONS"

BY

WILLIAM McDOUGALL

PROFESSOR OF PSYCHOLOGY IN HARVARD COLLEGE

NEW YORK
CHARLES SCRIBNER'S SONS
1921

THE SCRIBNER PRESS

FOREWORD

As I watch the American nation speeding gaily, with invincible optimism, down the road to destruction, I seem to be contemplating the greatest tragedy in the history of mankind. Other nations have declined and passed away; and their places have been filled, the torch of civilization has been caught up and carried forward by new nations emerging from the shadow-lands of barbarism. But, if the American nation should go down, whence may we expect a new birth of progress? Where shall we look for a virile stock fit to take up the tasks of world-leadership? It may be that the yellow millions of the Far East contain the potency of an indefinite progress and stability. That is a vague and uncertain possibility. Whatever that potency may be, it behooves us, the bearers of Western civilization, to take most anxious thought that we may prevent, if possible, the decline and decay which have been the fate of all the civilized nations of Europe and of the Near and Middle East.

Many excellent books have been published,

urging the claims of "eugenics," since Francis
Galton first stirred the conscience of Europe and
America on this problem of the preservation of
human qualities. Most of these books have been
written from the purely biological standpoint.
They give excellent accounts of the principles of
natural selection, of heredity, and of the Mendelian laws. It has seemed to me that a presen-
tation of the case for eugenics from a more psychological standpoint and on a broad historical
background might usefully supplement these biological treatises. For, important as are the facts
and principles of physical heredity, the general
reader may have some difficulty in connecting the
processes of cell-division, the chromosomes of the
fruit-fly, or the coat-colors of piebald guinea-pigs
with the spiritual endowment of mankind. I have
therefore brought together in these few lectures
the findings of mental anthropology, which are
now beginning to be garnered on a large scale;
and I have tried to indicate, in as impartial and
scientific a manner as is possible in this still obscure field, their bearing upon the great problems
of national welfare and national decay. The body
of the book is the substance of six lectures given
at the Lowell Institute of Boston in the spring of
this year. I have added in foot-notes some evi-

dential matter which may be neglected by the cursory reader. And in appendices I have put forward certain proposals which, if they could be put into practice, would, I think, go far to remedy the present disastrous state of affairs.

I would especially draw the attention of readers interested in political, economic, or social science to the evidence cited in this volume which indicates very strongly, if it does not finally prove, that the social stratification which exists in modern industrial communities is positively correlated with a corresponding stratification of innate moral and intellectual quality, or, in less technical language, that the upper social strata, as compared with the lower, contain a larger proportion of persons of superior natural endowments. This is a proposition which has been stoutly maintained by most of the eugenists from Galton onward. But it has been the greatest weakness of the eugenic propaganda that it is so largely founded upon and assumes the truth of this proposition. For the critics and scorners of eugenics have vehemently denied it, or poured ridicule upon it; and no proof of it was available for their refutation. In a paper read before the Eugenics Education Society in London ("Psychology in the Service of Eugenics," *Eugenics Review*, January, 1914) I pointed out that this great gap in the eugenist argument could only be filled by applying the methods of experimental psychology. Two of my pupils (Mr. C. Burt and Mr. H. B. English) made the first contribution by such methods toward the filling of the gap; and more recently several similar studies with similar positive results have been made in this country. They are reported in the following pages.

W. McD.

Harvard College,
April, 1921.

IS AMERICA
SAFE FOR DEMOCRACY?

IS AMERICA SAFE FOR DEMOCRACY?

I

In this short course of lectures I propose to direct your attention to a most difficult and obscure question. I have chosen this difficult topic, not because I have any new or startling conclusions to announce, but because the facts and reflections I am to put before you have urgent bearing upon many problems of private conduct and public policy. The importance of our topic is very great for all peoples; but for the American people at the present time it seems to me to overshadow and dwarf every other that any man of science could propose for your consideration. Why has it this supreme importance at this time and place? Because you, the American people, are laying the foundations of the American nation, a nation which already outstrips every other in its influence upon, or its capacity of influencing, the future history of mankind. You may still have rivals in the fields of art and science and literature. There are peoples more numerous than you; and there are states which control greater areas of the earth's surface and larger masses of population. But in two respects you stand unrivalled. First, in respect of the number of persons among you who are brought under the higher influences of that civilization which now controls the world, and which, if human foresight is not wholly untrustworthy, promises to be the foundation of all future civilization, no matter how great the changes it may undergo. Secondly, the American people is unrivalled in respect of the material resources which it effectively controls as the essential basis of its power and culture in the present and of its progress in the future.

The great increase of knowledge which we owe to the scientific labors of the nineteenth century has put us, the bearers of the civilization of the twentieth century, in a position that has no precedent, a position profoundly different from that of any of the great civilizations of the past. The Romans, the Greeks, the Persians, the Egyptians, the Babylonians, were surrounded by unknown possibilities; their vision was confined to a small area of the earth and to their own immediate past. To foresee their future or to control it was for them wholly impossible. How different is our position! We have mapped the whole earth; we know its status and relations among the other heavenly bodies; we can describe, in a general way, its past history during many millions of years; we understand in some degree all the physical energies, and can in a large measure control them and bend them to the service of mankind. All the races of men are known to us. There remains no great reservoir of humankind which may issue from some uncharted region to overwhelm and destroy our civilization. And, most important of all, we are beginning to understand something of the nature of man, something of the history of the development of the species, something of our bodily frame and mental powers, and of the long process by which our intellectual and moral culture has been achieved.

The Great War has given us one new item of knowledge which completes our assurance that we, the heirs of Western civilization, hold its destiny in our hands to make or mar. Before the war it was an open question whether civilized man, bred largely in towns to sedentary modes of life, could sustain the hardships and strains of prolonged warfare; whether in a clash of arms against some more primitive people we might not be overborne and swept away for sheer lack of nerve, of animal courage; whether our town-bred bespectacled young men, their imaginations quickened by education, and all unused to physical hardship, pain, and bloodshed, might not shrink and crumble when brought face to face with the horrors of war. But in the terrible years we have lived through we have seen regiments of cockneys from the London suburbs, and of Lancashire lads drawn from the mills and factories of the world's greatest industrial hive, distinguish themselves by gallantry and by patient courage in the field. These men have remained resolute and cheerful under a strain of warfare which, in respect of its horrors, its intense physical and emotional shocks, and the long continuance of the strain, has far surpassed every previous and more primitive warfare. We know now that civilization and culture, even in their worst forms, do not necessarily sap the moral energies of men; rather, we know that trained intelligence and disciplined will can withstand the extreme horrors of war far better than the cruder more animal courage of the primitive hunter and warrior.

Our civilization stands, then, in this position of immense advantage as compared with all civilizations of the past. And on the American people lies the responsibility for its future in a greater degree than on any other; because it has at its command, in a higher degree than any other, all the resources, material and spiritual, from which our civilization proceeds.

I will state concisely the thesis which I shall develop and attempt to prove to you in this course of lectures. Looking back over the history of mankind, we see that it consists in the successive rise and decay of great civilizations borne by different peoples in various parts of the earth. I need not enumerate these; their names are familiar to you. The facts have been insisted upon by many writers; they have been displayed by none more clearly than by Professor Flinders Petrie in his "Revolutions of Civilization." They are summed up in the familiar phrase, "cycles of civilization." They are briefly as follows. We see again and again a people in some favored area of the earth's surface slowly build up a great and complex civilization, incorporating essential elements of culture which it has acquired from some older civilization, adding to them and moulding them into harmony with its own genius and special needs. For many centuries the slow process of upbuilding, growth, and enrichment goes on. Then comes an arrest and, usually after a comparatively short period, the whole complex organism decays and plunges more or less rapidly downward from the height it had attained. In some cases the decay has gone so far that nothing remains of the people and its culture, beyond a few mounds of earth and broken brick. In others the people has continued to exist, but stagnant and inert, contributing nothing further to the progress of mankind, retaining little or nothing of what was most admirable in its period of ascent and greatness.

It is as though each such people, having been projected upon its upward path by some great force, maintains its ascending movement until its momentum is spent, then falls back to earth, a mere mass of human clay, undistinguished above others by any power to create, to progress, or in any way rise above the common level of mankind. If we seek a phrase which will convey most concisely the nature of this recurring process, the process which has been denoted by the phrase "revolutions or cycles of civilization," we may, I suggest, best describe it as "the parabola of peoples." For the course of the rise and fall of a people tends to resemble the trajectory of a stone thrown obliquely upward from the hand, a long ascending curve, an almost flat summit, and a steep decline.

Many speculations have been provoked by the contemplation of this recurring phenomenon. The first response of the mind is to ask—Is this inevitable, is this parabola the expression of some inescapable law of nature? Are we also destined to follow the same curve and, sooner or later, to plunge downward to stagnation or decay? Or may we, by taking thought, hope to escape the common fate of all our predecessors? Can we establish our course so securely that our descendants may continue to progress, for an indefinitely long period, in art and science and social organization, attaining heights of power, security, and happiness unimaginable by us?

In order to answer these questions, we must have some understanding of the causes of the rise and fall of the curve of civilization. The answers that have been suggested fall into two main classes: first, the answer implied by the economic interpretation of history; secondly, the anthropological answer. The former would see the essential factors in changes of climate, discoveries of new sources of wealth or of energy, or the opening up of new regions of the earth and the consequent shiftings of trade routes. The anthropological theory regards all such economic factors as of but subsidiary importance. It points out that peoples which were destined to climb the curve have subdued and transformed the physical world to their needs or, if necessary, have sought out and conquered for themselves a more propitious habitat. It points to regions such as Mesopotamia and the Nile valley, where men have made the desert bloom with all that was needed as the physical basis of great civilizations. And it points to other great regions, such as Africa south of the Sahara, and South and North America, regions which are richest in all that man needs and which nevertheless produced hardly more than savagery or barbarism, while Europe and Asia saw the rise and fall of many civilizations. It asserts also that in such regions as Mesopotamia and Egypt there have been no great changes (save such as man himself has produced) which could account for the rise or fall of their peoples. It points to the fact that the Roman Empire, which for four hundred years controlled the resources of the fairest regions of Europe, Northern Africa, and Asia, levying tribute upon all the known world, went down beneath the assault of the barbarians from the North, without any great change of economic conditions that can be assigned as a cause. Such instances show that the economic factors are of secondary importance; they show that the most favorable area can become the seat of a great civilization only when it is occupied by a people more capable than most of profiting by its geographic advantages; and that these advantages will not avail to save a people from decay, if and when it loses its natural superiority.

One anthropologic theory has been widely accepted as accounting for the decay of peoples. Leaving the problem of their ascent untouched, it asserts that peoples grow old, just as men and animals do, and that they must as inevitably decline in vigor after a certain age. It cannot be too strongly insisted that this fatalistic theory is utterly unfounded, if it is offered as anything more than a descriptive formula.

Professor Flinders Petrie, who has brought out so clearly the facts we are considering, and who points out that the period of the cycle or parabola has approximated in many instances to one thousand eight hundred years, advances a theory which claims to explain both the rise and the fall of the curve. He supposes that every cycle is initiated by a biological blending of two races; that this gives to the blended stock a new energy which carries it up the scale of civilization; that, after about one thousand eight hundred years, this effect is exhausted and that, in consequence of loss of vigor, decline inevitably sets in.

There may be some truth in this view as regards the initiation of the rise of a civilization. There is some evidence that the crossing of closely related stocks does conduce to increase of vigor and probably also to variability; and that these effects must be favorable to national progress seems obvious. Vigor, energy of mind and body, is certainly an all-important factor, without which all other natural endowments and advantages will effect little. And variability of the stock would seem to be a necessary condition of the production of the persons of exceptional endowments without whom a nation can neither rise in the scale of civilization nor maintain a great position.

But as regards the decline of peoples, Petrie's theory seems to contain less of truth. The old view that inbreeding necessarily results in degeneration has been much blown upon of late. Facts are accumulating which seem to show that very close inbreeding is compatible with continued and even increased vigor of the stock.

Now, it is this second part of the problem in which we are practically interested. We belong to a stock which has produced a great civilization, one which seems to be still on the ascending part of its curve. Our concern, our responsibility, is to maintain if possible that ascending curve, or at least to postpone as long as possible the onset of the period of decline, if that, in truth, must inevitably come. And there are not lacking indications that our Western civilization may already have reached its climax, may even now be sliding down the curve of decline. For we must not allow ourselves to be dazzled by the material, achievements of the recent past. In trying to estimate our position, we must have regard to moral and intellectual achievements of kinds less easily appreciated than the aeroplane and the big gun, the submarine and the poison-gas.

It is true that we have obtained a wonderful command over the physical energies of the world; but if we have not, individually and collectively as nations, the wisdom, the patience, the self-control, to direct these immense energies conformably to high moral ideals, our tampering with them will but hasten our end, will but plunge us the more rapidly down the slope of destruction. There is but too good ground for the fear that our knowledge has outrun our wisdom, that, though we have learned to exploit the physical energies of the world, we have not the wisdom and morality effectively to direct them for the good of mankind.

Leaving, then, the obscure problem of the origins of civilizations and of the causes of the ascent of peoples, I wish to concentrate your attention upon the more urgent and practically important problem of the causes or conditions that bring about their decline. In respect of this great problem, my thesis is that the anthropological theory is the true one, *that the great condition of the decline of any civilization is the inadequacy of the qualities of the people who are the bearers of it.*

This inadequacy may be one of two kinds; or it may be, perhaps generally has been, of both kinds. Inadequacy of the one kind may result from the increase of complexity of the environment which accompanies the rise of civilization, which is, in fact, an inevitable and necessary feature of it. Without change of the essential qualities of a people, those qualities may become relatively inadequate to the support of its civilization; just because advancing civilization makes, with every step of progress, greater demands upon its bearers. Let me illustrate by reference to three great features which, in various degrees, appear in all civilizations. First, increasing control of natural resources gives men leisure and opportunity to seek relaxation and amusement. Now leisure and amusement are most dangerous things, as some of us know. Few men are capable of using leisure and of choosing their amusements entirely wisely, and some men are quite incapable of doing so. Well, civilization inevitably lays upon great masses of men this responsibility. How do they respond to it? We know how in the great age of Rome the circus, the combat of gladiators and of wild beasts, and the chariot races, became the passionate delight of the multitude. We know how many forms of luxury, wines, perfumes, foods, baths, slaves, with resulting habits of indulgence, were introduced from all parts of the world. Under such complexities of environment many men who, under simpler conditions, would have lived solid, useful, and happy lives, became enervated, their interests and leisure increasingly absorbed in these useless if not actually harmful amusements.

Secondly, the increase of complexity of personal relations tends also to demand ever higher qualities from the persons concerned. Consider the relations of employer and workman. In the days of slavery, whether in Greece or Rome or Virginia, how simple were the qualities required for the satisfactory working of the institution, the relation! The owner of an estate worked by slaves had only to be an intelligent and kind-hearted man in order to be surrounded by happy faithful workers, a benevolent autocrat in the midst of grateful and devoted followers. And in the intermediate stage of small farming and small industry, where the employer is in close personal contact with all his men, a small dose of kindliness and good sense goes a long way to the maintenance of satisfactory relations. But to-day, in our industrial world, what great demands are made on the qualities of the employer! How patient, how understanding, how far-sighted, how humane he must be, if he is to avoid bitter strife with his work-people!

Thirdly, and perhaps most important, the in-creased intercourse between peoples, which is a leading feature and condition of progressing civ-ilization, inevitably weakens, when it does not altogether destroy, the influence of the customs and moral traditions by which our lives are guided. Instead of being moulded insensibly to conform to the customs and traditions which have sufficed to bring our forefathers safely through the perils of life, to guide them in the simpler environment of the past, we are confronted by ever more numerous possibilities of choice be-

tween rival customs and traditions and new beliefs and theories. We are called upon to choose
wisely, to steer our course warily, among untried
but perhaps attractive novelties, new religions,
new social theories, new ethical precepts. And
the result of all this is inevitable; it is the price
that must be paid for progress; not only do the
customs and traditions to which each man ad-
heres exert a less powerful sway over his conduct,
but also the harmony of the society in which and
by which he lives is weakened and disordered.

In these ways, and in many others, every advance of civilization makes greater demands upon
the qualities of its bearers; and it is, I think, obvious that in these respects our present civilization has surpassed all its predecessors, surpassed
them in the opportunities for leisure and amusement, in the complexity of personal relations, in
the variety of customs, traditions, beliefs, theories
of conduct, with which we are brought in contact, all demanding on our part the exercise of a
wisdom, a self-control, and a degree of devotion
to a moral ideal, such as no previous civilization
has required.

We are making great efforts to meet these demands, we are multiplying and improving our
educational institutions; and, in this country es-

pecially, the rising generation seems to be respond-
ing, by making full use of the advantages provided
for it.   But there remains to be answered the all-
important question—Is it possible, by improved
and extended education, adequately to prepare
the rising generations for the immense responsibilities they must bear? Are their innate qualities
such as will enable them to rise to the level required by the increasing complexity and difficulty
of the tasks that will be laid upon them? Will
the human qualities which have carried our civilization upward to its present point of complexity
—will they suffice to carry it further, or even to
maintain it at its present level?

That is a grave question. But a still graver
question calls for our most earnest consideration,
namely: Does not progressive civilization, while it
makes ever greater demands on the qualities of
its bearers, does it not tend to impair, has it not
always in the past actually impaired, the qualities
of the peoples on whom it makes these increasing
demands?

History and Anthropology seem to point to the
same answer to this grave question—namely, to
the positive answer. History seems to exhibit
unmistakably this tendency of civilization to impair the qualities of its bearers; and Anthropology

shows us how and why it has so worked in the
past and still is tending, perhaps more strongly
than ever before, in this direction.

Here, then, is the anthropological theory of the
decline of peoples:

Every human being, and therefore every community of human beings, every populace, inherits
from its ancestry a stock of innate qualities which
enable it to enjoy, to sustain, to promote, a civilization of a certain degree of complexity. As
civilization advances, it makes greater and greater
demands on these qualities, requires their exercise and development in ever fuller degree; until
it approaches a point at which its complexity out-
runs the possibilities of the innate qualities. At
the same time it tends positively to impair those
qualities; so that, as the demands increase, the
latent reserves of human quality are diminished.
Therefore a time comes when the supply no
longer equals the demand; that moment is the
culminating point of that civilization and of that
people, the turning-point of the curve from which
the downward plunge begins. This downward
tendency may be gradual and difficult to discern
at first; but History seems to show that it is apt
to be an accelerating process.

Anthropology is the latest and most backward

of the sciences. The proper study of mankind is man. But how difficult is that study! It is not very difficult to study the things that man has made, his languages, his arts, his manufactures, his social organizations, his achievements of all kinds. But how difficult to infer from these the nature of man's constitution! How difficult to correlate any peculiarities in these products of his activities with any peculiarities of natural endowment! The physical anthropologists have, during the last half-century, accumulated a vast mass of data about certain of his bodily qualities —the proportions of his skull and other bones, the color of his eyes, his stature and his complexion and his hair. These data are of great value; but they concern merely his material structure. It is the mental constitution of man, the varying sum of his mental qualities, that is alone of direct importance and with which we are concerned. The bodily peculiarities are of importance chiefly in so far as they may serve as indicators of mental qualities. It is this mental anthropology which is so difficult a study that it has only quite recently begun to take shape as a science, the science we call modern psychology. And that science is, accordingly, in a very rudimentary condition, hopeful and active, but still the scene of the most widely divergent views in respect of its fundamental questions. Especially as regards the innate basis of the human mind, we still have little light and much difference of opinion. Yet only knowledge of the innate basis of the mind will enable us to arrive at well-founded views, in face of the great problems of the rise and fall of nations.

No wonder, then, that, when these problems began to be actively debated early in the last century, there were acute differences of opinion, much error and much false dogma. For not only was all such discussion carried on in the total absence of the necessary basis of knowledge, but it was a discussion in which the participants almost inevitably were moved by strong desires other than the desire for truth, in which judgment was distorted by strong prejudices and sentiments. The debate inevitably raised the question of the relative values of the human races, the superiority or inferiority of this race to that, of one people to another. In the absence of all certain knowledge of the fundamental facts, what hope was there that racial bias should be discounted and kept in check?

The story opens with the myth of the Aryan race. This "race" was a phantasy erected by racial prejudice on a basis of the study of languages. Community of language was accepted, in the face of all probability, as evidence of community of race. And the learned world was convulsed with controversies over the origin of the Aryans, a race which had never existed. From the first, racial prejudice was at work; for the Aryans were conceived as the race which had produced all that was most esteemed in the culture of Europe and of Asia; and, from the first, the whole question was confused by the search for the lost ten tribes of Israel. The errors of this early stage of the discussion provoked some of the most influential writers of the middle of last century to repudiate the notion of differences of mental constitution between the races of men. J. S. Mill declared: "Of all vulgar modes of escaping from the consideration of the effect of social and moral influences on the human mind, the most vulgar is that of attributing the diversities of conduct and character to inherent natural differences." And he was followed by many others. For at that time the prevailing view of the human mind, of which Mill was the chief exponent, was all against the assumption of racial differences; and the prevailing humanitarian sentiment, of which also Mill was a leading exponent, made strongly in the same direction. The psychology of that time was the "Association psychology" that had come down from Locke and Hume. It taught that at birth the human mind is a blank sheet, and the brain a structureless mass, lacking all inherent organization or tendencies to develop in this way or that; a mere mass of undefined potentialities which, through experience, association, and habit, through education in short, could be moulded and developed to an unlimited extent and in any manner or direction.

There prevailed, therefore, at that time a profound belief in the unlimited power of education. J. S. Mill himself had been most carefully educated from his earliest years by his father; and he attributed his own achievements in the intellectual sphere wholly to that fact, overlooking a still more important fact, namely, that he was the son of his father, a man of great intellectual vigor and capacity. Even those who perceived the truth that by education you cannot make every child into a great man believed, nevertheless, that the educative process had only to be applied to some few successive generations, in order to raise any people or any human stock to an indefinite degree in the scale of intellectual and moral value.

Humanitarian sentiment worked powerfully in

favor of this theory of the unlimited power of education. For there is something cold and cruel, something repugnant to the natural kindliness of the normal man, in the opposite theory, the theory that some men, and even whole races of men, are born incapable of being educated beyond a very modest level of intellectual and moral achievement. We should all like to agree with the member of the British Parliament who, indignantly repudiating an aspersion cast upon some section of his countrymen, declared that "one man is as good as another—and a great deal better too, sometimes."

So striking are the immediate effects of education, and so strong is the influence of humanitarian feeling upon opinion, that this confidence in the unlimited power of education still prevails in the popular mind; it is, I think, the basis of much of the fine optimism with which the American people confronts its tasks, the implicit theory on which your practice is based.[1]

Yet, since the day of Mill, science has done much that saps this theory; it has achieved new

---

[1] For example, I am told by a prominent educationist that America is engaged in levelling up the Philippines to her own standards by instituting universal and compulsory schooling among them.

knowledge which, if it were generally understood, would go far to undermine the complacency with which the popular mind contemplates the future.

This new insight into the nature of man forbids us scornfully to set aside, as the vulgar errors of the "race-theorizers," all attempts to estimate the intrinsic values, the cultural potentialities, of different human stocks. It calls upon us to weigh the evidence most carefully and impartially, putting aside, as strictly as in us lies, both racial prejudice and humanitarian sentiment; to recognize that, if Nature has made men of unequal value, the cruelty is hers, not ours, and that we do no wrong in ascertaining and recording the facts.

The framers of The Declaration of Independence embodied in it the celebrated proposition that "all men are created equal." There are two senses in which this sentence may be interpreted. It may be taken to mean that all men are equal in respect of their claims for justice, for humane treatment and the kindly feeling of their fellows, for opportunities to make the best of their powers of service and of happiness. On the other hand, it may be, and sometimes has been, taken to mean that all men are born with equal capacities for intellectual and moral development. There can be no doubt, I think, that the former interpretation is the true one. The untruth of the second interpretation is so obvious, and in all ages has been so obvious, that we do wrong to the great men who framed the proposition, if we assume that the second meaning was intended by them. In the former sense the proposition conveys a great moral truth and a moral ideal which all men can accept as a fundamental principle of conduct.

II

ABOUT the time at which J. S. Mill denounced
the vulgar errors of the race-theorizers, and at
which T. H. Buckle, the historian of civilization
in Europe, claimed to show that the peoples of
the various regions of the earth are moulded by
their physical environments like so much soft clay,
the theory of the all-importance of race took a
new turn and gave rise to a school of thought
which has flourished greatly, which still flourishes,
and which has produced great and disastrous historical effects.

In 1854 Count Gobineau published his treatise
on the "Inequality of the Races of Man," and
thereby founded the German school of race-dogmatists, sometimes called the school of politico-
anthropology. He announced to the world: "I
have become convinced that everything in the
way of human creation, science, art, civilization,
all that is great and noble and fruitful on the
earth, points toward a single source, is sprung
from one and the same root, belongs only to one
family, the various branches of which have dominated every civilized region of the world." This

family he asserted to be the Teutonic race. Gobineau's race-theory chimed so well with the political aspirations of the leaders of Germany that, with appropriate modification to the effect that the modern Germans are the purest representatives of the super-race, it became the official doctrine of that country. It was adopted and propagated assiduously by a multitude of men, both great and small. Richard Wagner was one of the ardent disciples of this school. Nietzsche's conception of a "great blond beast" of a superman gave the dogma a literary expression which profoundly influenced many young Germans. German anthropologists busied themselves to discover evidence in its support. H. S. Chamberlain, popularly known as the Kaiser's favorite anthropologist, gave it its most complete expression in his "Foundations of the 19th Century," a book which greatly influenced the Germans, from Wilhelm II downward. In these ways, by means of this conspiracy officially promoted for the perversion of the truth, the German people, docile as always to their elaborately organized system of official instruction, was persuaded to believe, against the evidence of most obvious facts, that it was the chosen people of the world. And the acceptance of this race-dogma did much

to convince the leaders and the masses of the
German people that they were morally justified
in setting out in 1914 to exterminate their weaker
neighbors, as a first and necessary step to that
world-rulership to which they believed themselves
to be destined by Nature or by God. And the
professors, if we may judge by many utterances,
including the infamous manifesto signed by ninety-
three of the most prominent of them, were just
as suggestible and deluded as the masses. This
dogma of the natural and predestined supremacy
of the German people gave rise incidentally, but
inevitably, to a polemic against the Jews, and
greatly promoted the crusade of the Anti-Semites.
For the Jews had long claimed to be the chosen
people of the Lord; and their remarkable persistence as a people, in spite of all adverse influences, and, it may be added, their remarkable
achievements, lent some color to this view. Thus
the race-dogma accentuated racial hatreds and
international hostilities. Odious as all this was,
it had one good effect. It stimulated some men,
more especially a number of capable Jews, to examine in a critical spirit the evidence on which
the race-dogma claimed to be founded.

Notable among these are Friedrich Hertz,
author of "Modern Race Theories," and Ignaz

Zollshan, whose book, "The Race Problem," published in 1909, is a critical examination of the German race-dogma and a temperate and successful defense of the racial value of the Jews. These writers had no difficulty in exposing to impartial readers the exaggerations and distortions of the German race-dogmatists. The logic of the latter was deplorable, and their disregard of facts was obvious to the most casual reader. It was their habit to discover some traces of physical qualities, such as tall stature, blue eyes, long heads, or fair hair, among whatever people had achieved any noteworthy work, and, taking this as evidence of some infusion of Germanic blood, to attribute the achievement of that people wholly to this alleged strain in the population concerned.

I will not delay to expose their methods and the falsity of their claims. I will merely point out that a less extreme and more defensible form of this race-theory still finds many supporters. Dr. C. Woodruff,[1] and Mr. Madison Grant,[2] in this country, De Lapouge[3] in France, are examples. They claim an intrinsic and great superiority, not

---

[1] "The Expansion of Races."
[2] "The Passing of the Great Race."
[3] "Les Sélections Sociales."

for the Germans or the Teutons, but for the Nordic race of Europe, which is represented in Germany, it is true, but not so strongly as in other areas. Anthropologists are now pretty well agreed that this Nordic race really did exist, and that, mixed in various proportions, its blood is still widely represented in various parts of the world. Without claiming for it any general innate superiority, we may fairly inquire whether it possessed and still exhibits any human qualities in peculiar degree or combination. But, before passing to examine the evidence for differences of natural endowment, let us glance at the arguments of those who to-day represent the school of Mill, denying all differences of mental endowment, or regarding them as so slight as to be negligible factors in world-history.

Of the many critics of the race-dogmatists, I will cite only the names of M. J. Finot, author of "The Prejudices of Race," of Mr. J. M. Robertson, the vindicator of Buckle, and of Mr. J. Oakesmith. Mr. Oakesmith's book on "Race and Nationality" (1919) is the latest important work. on this side of the argument and well represents the rest. These authors, who deny all importance to racial composition and differences of innate endowment, may conveniently be classed over against their opponents, the race-dogmatists, as the "race-slumpers." It is characteristic of them that they in the main avoid the straight issue and content themselves with exposing the errors of the race-dogmatists. They make much of the undeniable truth that none of the civilized peoples of the world are of pure race, but rather are all alike the products of repeated blendings of races and peoples. They point out that, if any racial peculiarities of mental constitution exist, they are so obscure that no one has been able to define them and measure them, as the physical anthropologists have succeeded in defining and measuring certain physical qualities as indicators of race. They point to the fact that in many instances men born of primitive and even savage parents have shown themselves capable of acquiring all the elements of culture of the most highly civilized communities, and of playing an honorable part in the complex life of such a community. They delight in telling us how the native children in this or that missionary school excel their white fellows in learning the A B C, or even in acquiring the three R's. Especially they avoid the direct issue by demonstrating at length the obvious truth that race and nationality are not coincident. This is merely a red herring drawn across the track, to put us off the scent. The "race-slumpers" have shown, it must be admitted, that the facile generalizations of many historians upon race and national character have been of the most flimsy nature, often erroneous and sometimes absurd. We must recognize with them that these flimsy assumptions have worked harm; and we must agree with them in condemning in the most outspoken way the evil work of the more extreme race-dogmatists.[1]

But when Mr. Oakesmith concludes that the practical value of "race" is purely subjective; that "race" is merely an emotion, like that of the soldier who is proud of his regiment's history; when the "race-slumpers" assert or imply, as they do, that all men are born with the same mental endowments, that all human stocks are of equal value, and that the anthropologic composition of a people is of no influence upon the course of its history, then we must part company from them. These writers have shown that the training of the pure historian does not qualify him to propound

---

[1] Oakesmith (p. 58) says of Chamberlain's work: "It is false in its theories; ludicrously inaccurate in its assertions; pompous and extravagant in its style; insolent to its critics and opponents." With these strictures I entirely agree.

sweeping generalizations about racial qualities; and that, when he undertakes to do so, in entire ignorance of the findings of anthropology and equipped only with the fallacious psychology which is embodied in common speech, he cannot hope to arrive at the truth. They have shown that the historian, if he would rightly interpret or explain the course of the history of peoples, rather than be content merely to describe it, must go to school with the anthropologists, must take account of all their findings, and must wait patiently until we shall have accumulated more data and a surer insight into that obscurest and most difficult of all problems with which science is concerned—the mental constitution of man and its subtle variations.

In all this question of race and nationality we need, in short, to make a new start. Instead of throwing ourselves passionately into one or other of the opposed camps, the camp of the race-dogmatists or that of the race-slumpers, we must examine the evidence afresh with strict impartiality, unmoved by national prejudice or by humanitarian sentiment. Especially we must disentangle and clearly distinguish between national character and racial or ethnic qualities. For the confusion of these conceptions has been

the root of most of the trouble. National character, as I have taken some pains to show,[1] is not
the mere sum or average of individual characters or qualities. But that is not to say that individual qualities play no part in shaping national
character. Both parties have made the mistake
of regarding national character as the sum or
average of individual qualities; the race-dogmatists assuming that the nation in all its doings
always expresses certain individual qualities,
which they assume to be common to all members
of the nation; the race-slumpers pointing out in
return that, at different periods of its history, a
nation exhibits itself in very different characters;
for example, they point out that the Jews were at
one time an agricultural and warlike people, but
that in modern times they have seemed very
averse from both agriculture and war; and they
deduce from such facts the conclusion that the
qualities of any population are completely fluid
and indefinite.

It will, I think, help us to define our problem
more exactly, if we state it concretely in the fol-

---

[1] "The Group Mind. A Sketch of the Principles of
Collective Psychology, with Some Attempt to Apply
Them to the Interpretation of National Life and Char-
acter." New York, 1920.

lowing way.[1] Let us imagine that in some one of
the great well-defined nations—say the British—
every infant, throughout a period of fifty years,
could be exchanged without the knowledge of its
parents for an infant of another people. If this
were done, at the close of the period of fifty
years the anthropologic constitution of the nation
would have been completely changed or exchanged.
Would that affect the future course of its national
life? If so, in what manner and degree? If we
suppose the exchange to have been made with some
other nation of similar composition and level of
culture, the race-slumpers—Messrs. Finot, Oakesmith, Robertson—would confidently reply: "No,
it would make no difference." Would they give
the same reply if the exchange were made with
some remoter people, say the Japanese, or Ar-
menians, or Italians; or with a still remoter people, say the Hottentots or the Bushmen of
southern Africa, or the Malays of the Far East?
Their principles logically would compel them to
give the same reply; but I fancy that, when confronted with the issue in this concrete form, the
most extreme of them would hesitate to do so.

[1] As I did some twelve years ago in my "Introduction
to Social Psychology," p. 330, fifteenth edition, Boston,
1920.

They would probably put us off with some reference to physical incompatibility of climate, and so forth. For these writers do not and cannot deny important physical peculiarities of race; their negation applies only to differences of mental endowment, in respect of which the establishment of the facts is so much more difficult.

Let us see, then, what evidence we have bearing on this great question of differences of innate mental endowment. And we will begin with the problem of intellectual endowment, or innate capacity for the development of intellect or intelligence. For, though the moral factors may be more important, intelligence is a valuable quality and not to be despised; and it is more easily measurable than the moral qualities.

Let us notice first that in Anthropology we have to deal with human beings in mass, and have to treat our facts by statistical methods, as far as possible. Therefore the pointing to individual cases of the presence of well-marked qualities, even if such cases be numerous, is out of order, and merely confuses the issue. Consider this for a moment in relation to a simply measured physical quality, say stature. When the anthropologist asserts that one population, A, is shorter than another, B, he is speaking of averages; he

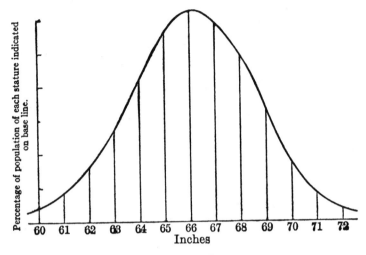

FIGURE I

A normal curve of distribution of stature in a population, the average stature of which is 66 inches.

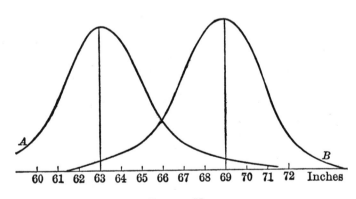

FIGURE II

The overlapping curves of distribution of stature in two homogeneous populations of which one (A) has the average stature of 63 inches, the other (B) 69 inches.

does not mean to deny that tall men may be found in A and short men in B; and to point to even extreme instances of such aberration from the average does not invalidate his generalization. If the two populations contrasted are fairly homogeneous, the statures of each may be represented roughly by a curve, the abscissæ of which represent the various heights, each ordinate the percentage of the population which has the height marked on the horizontal line. These are the normal curves of distribution. Or if one population is mixed or formed by the intermarriage of two stocks of unequal stature, it may show a double peak.[1] In either case the average stature is a significant figure; and the generalization remains valid, even though you point to very tall men among A and to short men among B. In considering mental qualities, we must keep this way of viewing the facts constantly in mind, and must avoid the fallacy of seeking to upset

---

[1] Such a double-peaked curve would result if the two populations represented by the curves A and B of Fig. II were mixed, and the measurements of stature of a large sample of the mixed population were plotted on a single curve. Such double-peaked curves of physical qualities have been found, e. g., the curve of distribution of the cephalic index among the Greeks of Asia Minor (Ripley, "Races of Europe," p. 116).

generalizations by pointing to exceptional instances.

The example of stature is instructive by analogy in another way. When two populations are found to differ in average stature, we are not justified in assuming forthwith that this difference expresses a difference of innate constitution. We must inquire first into the conditions under which the two populations live. If A lives in an infertile area, under conditions of hardship and poor nutrition, its lower stature may be due to this fact. For there are clear instances in which low stature of a whole population may be traced to such causes. Only if the conditions are favorable to the full development of stature in both groups, does difference of the average stature imply difference of innate constitution. But, when such influences have been taken into account and allowed for, it appears clearly that the stature of men, or the extent of their growth in stature, is, even under the most favorable conditions, determined and limited by innate constitution. By taking thought a boy may add a little to his stature, but the amount he may so add is strictly limited. Further, stature is hereditary. Here again the statement is true statistically; and the statistical generalization is not invalidated by instances of tall sons born of short parents. What we mean by the statement is that, on the average, the sons of short forefathers will be, under equally good conditions, shorter than the sons of tall forefathers. Now, apply these ways of thinking to mental qualities, and we shall find evidence that intellectual stature and intellectual growth are subject to generalizations very similar to those which are found to hold good for physical stature and physical growth. This is an all-important thesis, fundamental to our whole problem.

The "race-slumpers," in their denial, both explicit and implied, of all significant differences between one man and another as regards mental qualities, are the champions of common sense and the views of the plain man—views in which the plain man has been supported by both law and medicine until very recent years. For the plain man, and law and medicine also, accepted the traditional assumption that our mental powers are the expression of a supernatural principle, the soul, miraculously implanted in each one of us at birth; and, while they recognized great differences of bodily endowment, they ignored comparable differences of mental endowment, with certain exceptions. The man of genius on the one hand, the idiot and the madman on the other hand, were mysterious exceptions; but, apart from these exceptions, all men were born equal, and all differences of attainment were attributed to differences of opportunity and education; all men had equal powers and equal responsibilities, and must be treated as strictly alike, unless their departure from the average was so extreme that they might claim to be men of genius, madmen, or idiots. Of such cases common sense, the law, and medicine washed their hands, disclaiming all responsibility —for they did not fit into the theory; the genius was allowed to go his own way, the madmen and idiots were handed over to special institutions and there secluded.

Very recently a step forward has been made in this connection. Medical men have recognized that idiots, the poor creatures whose defect of intellect is so great as to be obvious, as it were, to the naked eye, are not sharply marked off as a class from their fellow men. They have sought and found many transitional forms which connect the idiot with the normal or average man; and they have devised appropriate terms by which to denote those who approximate in various degrees to the condition of the idiot. The law has come to their help and has constituted a class of "mental defectives," persons whose intellectual capaci-

ties are so poor that they cannot be regarded as
fully responsible, but who must, for their own
sakes, be put into special schools and institutions;
because they cannot profit by the educational processes provided for the normal child, cannot com-
pete on even terms with the normal man. In these
schools and institutions they have been carefully
studied, and the following facts fully established.
Many of them differ greatly from the idiot (who
generally has defects of brain and body obvious
to the eye) in that to the untrained observer they
appear to be normal persons; and their brains and
physical development, even to the skilled observer,
present no marked peculiarities. Nevertheless, do
what you will for these people, lavish upon them,
from their earliest infancy, all the skill and care
of specialists in medicine and education, and you
cannot make them into normal adults, fully responsible persons, capable of holding their own
in the world. The best of them, after being carefully trained and taught some simple trade, can
go out into the world and, under favorable conditions, can earn a living, marry and produce children, and lead more or less useful respectable
lives. Others (and there are all grades and no
sharp divisions) cannot be brought to this level;
if they are sent out into the world to lead the

normal life, they fail and become paupers, tramps, or hoboes; or they appear again and again in the police courts for trivial offenses. Others are so obviously defective that they cannot be allowed to attempt to lead the normal life; and they are kept, much to their own benefit, in the appropriate institutions, harmless and happy and often, in a limited way, useful. These people illustrate the truth of what I said in my first lecture of the increasing demands of civilization upon the qualities of its bearers. In earlier times and in simpler communities such people undoubtedly existed or exist; but under those simpler conditions their defects would not disqualify them for the common life. In a simple rural community they may rub along fairly well. The mental defect of these persons, their defect of intelligence, is, then, not due to lack of education or opportunity; it is an inborn constitutional defect.

A second great fact has been established by the modern study of these mental defectives—namely, that their defect is not only inborn, or innate; it is also hereditary. In most cases it is inherited from similar parents or grandparents; and, if they produce children, it is likely to be transmitted to some or all of them. We do not yet fully understand the laws of its transmission; but one fact seems to be fully established: if two such defectives marry and produce children, all those children will also be "mental defectives."

In recent years an immense amount of study has been devoted to these cases by highly competent workers.[1] The facts as stated are established. No recitation of instances of boys who have risen to eminence from the gutter can shake them. May we suppose, then, that these mental defectives form a class sharply marked off from normal persons; as it used to be assumed that the idiots formed a class sharply marked off? Or is it possible that intelligence or intellectual stature closely resembles physical stature in respect of its distribution through the population? Evidence is fast accumulating to show that this view is true. An important step in mental anthropology has recently been made. The method of intelligence-tests (or mental testing) has been devised, and in the army and elsewhere has been assiduously applied. The methods have been proved on a scale which shows that the results achieved are "statistically" valid, though errors may and do occur in individual cases. Popular opinion of "mental

[1] See Doctor H. H. Goddard's "Human Efficiency and Levels of Intelligence," and his "Psychology of the Normal and Abnormal," Princeton, 1920.

testing" is naturally divided: those of us who did well when tested naturally think it a good system; those of us who did badly incline to the opinion that it is an absurd academic fad. But the evidence that its results are statistically valid is overwhelming.

I put before you a sample of the results obtained in the testing of a large batch (many thousands) of recruits from a given area. This particular sample (which I owe to the kindness of one of my pupils, Mr. N. D. Hirsch, who took part in the conduct of the testing) is especially interesting, because it includes both white and colored recruits, and because these were drawn from an area in which facilities for schooling were relatively poor, so that many of these recruits had enjoyed very

TABLE I

	A	B	C +	C	C −	D	D −	E
W. L....	2.6	6	12	26	23	28	0	0
W. I ...	.2	1.4	3.3	14	19	37	22	2
C. L....	1.0	1.4	3.1	9	19	39	26	0
C. I ...	.5	.3	.5	3.2	8	33	46	7

little schooling or none at all. The Table I shows the recruits arranged in four classes: white literates (W. L.), white illiterates (W. I.), colored literates

(C. L.), and colored illiterates (C. I.). The individuals of each of these classes are distributed in percentages under eight letters, in the order of decreasing intelligence.

There are many interesting features about this table. We see that each class taken by itself gives approximately an asymmetrical curve[1] of distribution of intelligence. The curves for the white illiterates and the colored literates run pretty closely together, indicating that these two classes show approximately the same degree of intelligence "statistically"; while the white literates' curve shows considerable shift to the left, and that of the colored illiterates a shift to the right.

You may be disposed at first sight to attribute the differences of intelligence disclosed to differences of degree of education, of schooling; but reflection shows that the assumption will not fit the facts.

First, the tests were deliberately designed in order to give no advantage to the more educated man as such. But, you may say, his education has made him more intelligent. Well, perhaps it has in some degree. But if education is the source

[1] The reader can easily picture for himself the curve of distribution implied by the figures for each of the four classes.

of the difference between the white literates and the white illiterates, and between the colored literates and the colored illiterates—what has made the difference between white and colored? Again, what makes the differences between the groups A to E in each class? They must be in the main native differences. A men occur in all classes. Further evidence of this may be seen in the nature of the curves. Each taken alone is asymmetrical. If we amalgamate the two curves for whites and the two curves for coloreds, we get curves nearer a normal curve of distribution. But both curves will still show a too abrupt descent on the right. This is partly accounted for if we remember that a certain number of young men were rejected at sight as obviously unfit to serve, including all the declared mental defectives. The addition of them would bring both curves nearer to the form of a normal symmetrical curve of distribution. Further, when a large group of college students were tested (three thousand men, all of whom had enjoyed the advantages of full school and some college education) they were found to spread out in a similar wide curve of widely different grades; the curve is not so wide as the curve representing all the whites of Table I, because the lower grades (D and E) are missing altogether. It resembles closely the curve for the white literates. Here the educational factor has been practically the same for all, yet the degrees of intellectual capacity as revealed by the tests are widely spread.

All these facts point to the one conclusion, namely, that innate capacity for intellectual growth is the predominant factor in determining the distribution of intelligence in adults, and that the amount and kind of education is a factor of subordinate importance.

The superiority of the white literates to the white illiterates is due, then, not wholly or mainly to their schooling, but rather to an inborn greater capacity for intellectual growth. Spontaneous selection has been at work in this region, where schooling is difficult to obtain; and, on the whole, those boys most fitted by nature to profit by schooling have obtained it. It must be noted that the class of illiterates includes many boys who attended school for a few years only and then dropped out. Does not common experience teach us that, where schooling is difficult to obtain, the brighter boys who find themselves making good progress in school are those who are most likely to continue at school? And is it not probable that the brighter boys and the sons of the more intelligent parents are more likely to enter school than the dullards and the sons of unintelligent parents?

Another point of interest is suggested by Table II, expressed in "mental age."[1] The difference

TABLE II

	Mental Age	Difference
W. L.	14.5 ⎱	2.3
W. I	12.2 ⎰	
C. L.	12.1 ⎱	1.5
C. I	10.6 ⎰	

ference between literates and illiterates is due partly to innate differences, partly to education; but the difference is much greater in whites than in coloreds. If we assume that the attraction of the schools works selectively in equal degree on whites and coloreds, and this seems a fair assumption, then it follows that the higher the level of innate capacity, the more is it improved by education.

Finally, when all the white recruits of the whole army are thrown into a single table, they give a curve conforming very closely to a normal curve of distribution.[2]

[1] A conventional scale in which the position of a very intelligent adult is expressed by the figure 20.
[2] See p. 37.

Such findings require confirmation by the more thorough testing of practical life, and they have had such thorough confirmation. For example, of a large group of college students who, after being tested, entered an officers' training-school, many were eventually rejected because they proved unfit to be officers. Of those who scored A or B in the tests at entry, eight-ninths passed through the school successfully; of those who scored C — or D, seven-eighths failed; of those who scored C, 50 per cent failed. Further, it was found that men who scored below C generally proved inadequate to the duties of a non-commissioned officer.

The official report, after carefully weighing all the evidence, states: "These examinations were intended, and are now definitely known, to measure native intellectual ability; they are to some extent influenced by educational acquirement, but in the main the soldier's inborn intelligence and not the accidents of environment determines his mental rating." [1]

---

[1] "Army Mental Tests," by P. S. Yoakum and R. M. Yerkes, 1920, p. 17. Professor S. M. Terman, who has had large experience in the application of mental tests to children, writes: "We are beginning to learn that all of these measures combined are powerless to reduce greatly

the number of over-age children in the grades. Notwithstanding the persistent campaign which has been waged against the evils of retardation for the last dozen years, the number of retardates remains to-day much the same as it was when the campaign began. . . . The facts . . . point fairly definitely to the conclusion that the differences which have been found to exist among children in physical traits are paralleled by equal differences in mental traits, particularly intelligence. It will be shown that these innate differences in intelligence are chiefly responsible for the problem of the school laggard." ("The Intelligence of School Children," p. 24.)

III

I have put before you evidence that in the population of this country innate intellectual capacity (or the capacity to develop intelligence) is continuously distributed, in much the same fashion as a physical quality such as stature. It is true that we cannot exactly define this vague thing which we measure and call "intellectual capacity." Is it a simple unitary factor which may be a Mendelian unit? Some psychologists, using a most ingenious statistical method (the method of correlation and the hierarchy), have argued that these various levels of intellectual capacity depend on the possession of more or less of such a single common factor, which they call general intelligence or "the G factor"; and they have proposed to call it "intellective energy." [1] You may object that this is a vague notion, and may ask—What exactly is this intellective energy? It is fair to reply that it is something

---

[1] *Cf.* especially papers by Professor C. Spearman, Mr. C. Burt, and others in the *British Journal of Psychology*, and Doctor Maxwell Garnet's "Education and World-Citizenship," London, 1921.

which we can measure and recognize, though we cannot describe it or adequately conceive it; and that in this respect it is just like electricity or other physical energies, which the engineer measures and controls but cannot fully understand or adequately describe. But, even if this is a mistaken view, and if the level of intellectual capacity is a resultant of many factors, that does not invalidate the conception for anthropological purposes. Physical stature (or the capacity to attain a certain stature) is a resultant of many factors (lengths of many bones), yet it is an inborn or innate quality; though affected by environment, yet it is determined by heredity; it is inborn in various degrees in individuals and in races, some having more and others less of it; and the same is true of intellectual capacity.

This conclusion is distasteful; for it sets a limit to the power of education. It may seem likely to discourage the enthusiasts of education; but it should not do that. Even though the effects of education are limited by Nature, it is of the highest importance that we make the most and the best of the human material which she supplies. Those who resent this limitation of the power of education are very apt to struggle against the conclusion by an argument of this kind. They describe instances of boys, taken from a deplorable environment and from undesirable parents, who, having been put under good conditions and given good education, have become useful or even distinguished citizens. But even a large number of such cases can do nothing to invalidate our conclusion. They may be set off completely by citing cases of the opposite type, cases of boys who, though denied every opportunity for schooling, nevertheless have attained to the very highest levels of distinction—boys like Abraham Lincoln or George Stephenson, the creator of the English railroads.

Let us look now a little more closely at the racial distribution of intellectual capacity. Unfortunately, facts are few, and, though I would rather choose for discussion any other race than the Negro, they alone of the colored peoples have been studied in a way which makes possible a comparison with the white population.

TABLE III

	A	B	C +	C	C −	D	D −	E
Whites....	2.0	4.8	9.7	20	22	30	8	2
Coloreds...	.8	1.0	1.9	6	15	37	30	7
Officers....	55.0	29.0	12.0	4	0	0	0	0

That races are endowed in different degrees with innate intellectual capacity is implied by the difference between the curves for whites and coloreds (Table III). We have seen that the curve for the colored literates almost coincides with that for the white illiterates. We have seen that the difference of level between the white literates and illiterates is determined in part by education, in part by natural endowment. Note, then, that whichever factor is predominant, or if either alone is responsible, the racial difference of native endowment stands out clearly.

Now, the colored men of this country are largely, I suppose, of mixed white and Negro descent. It may be suggested that the native inferiority of the colored in respect of this quality (intelligence) is an evil effect of the cross-breeding of these two widely dissimilar races. That is a possibility. But facts are strongly against it. First, the colored men of the Northern States showed distinct superiority to those of the South, in respect of their performance in the army intelligence-tests. Have they not a larger proportion of white blood? I do not know, but I suspect it.

Secondly, we have the fact that some of the leaders of the colored people deliberately advocate the improvement of the colored people by further miscegenation. A fact not conclusive, but a significant admission.

Thirdly, we have the allegation, frequently made, that every colored man who has risen to high distinction has been of mixed blood. It is perhaps difficult to prove the rule; but it is difficult to find exceptions.[1]

Fourthly, we have a few studies which suggest that, when two races of different intellectual capacity are crossed, the offspring are (statistically) intermediate, and that they approximate to the superior race according to the proportion of their blood derived from it.

As regards the Negro race, I know of no such study; probably the descent of the colored people cannot be traced with sufficient accuracy for this purpose.[2]

---

[1] The late Professor N. S. Shaler was a close student of the colored people, and was affectionately disposed toward them. In his book "The Neighbor" (Boston, 1904), which bears on every page the marks of the spirit of justice and benevolence, he states: "Almost all the Negroes of this country who have shown marked capacity of any kind have had an evident mixture of white blood" (p. 163). He mentions a single exception.

[2] Professor R. S. Woodworth, in an article on the "Comparative Psychology of Races" (*Psychological Bulletin*,

But we have two recent studies of Indians and cross-breeds of white and Indian blood, made quite independently by different observers and by different methods in different places. The Indians studied were all literates, pupils in Indian schools and colleges. The results of the two investigations agree. One observer[1] concludes that the Indians of mixed blood are superior in intellectual capacity to the full-blooded Indians by one full year of mental age. The other (Professor Hunter, University of Kansas) compared white children with Indians of full blood, and with those of one-quarter, one-half, and three-quarters of white blood; he shows that there is a large difference in

vol. XIII, 1916), summarizes the findings of three observers, all of whom, applying "intelligence-tests" to white and colored children, found the intellectual capacity of the coloreds to be (statistically) inferior to that of the whites. One of them (Ferguson) divided the colored children into four groups, according to the depth of coloration, and, accepting shade of color as an indication of the proportion of white blood, concluded, that "in the more intellectual tests, success increased with the proportion of white blood." Shaler wrote: "It is a common opinion, held by the blacks as well as the whites, that an infusion of white blood increases the intelligence of the Negro, while at the same time lowering his moral qualities." *Ibid.*, p. 162.

[1] Mr. T. R. Garth (University of Texas).

intellectual capacity between the white and the Indian, and that the cross-bred approximate to the white level in proportion to their share of white blood; and, after carefully considering all the possibilities, cautiously concludes that the difference is probably due to race.[1]

It seems highly probable, then, that the same rule holds good for the mulatto, and that, if pure Negroes were compared with whites, the difference of intellectual capacity would be considerably greater than that actually found between whites and coloreds.[2]

This conclusion is, I think, in harmony with the indications afforded by the whole history of the Negro race—not only in Africa and America, but in Oceania and especially in such regions as

[1] Summaries of the work of Mr. Garth and Mr. Hunter appear in the reports of the meeting of the American Psychological Association at Chicago, December, 1920 (*Psychological Bulletin*, 1921).

[2] In the *Journal of Applied Psychology* for 1919 Messrs. S. L. Pressey and G. F. Teter report "A Comparison of Colored and White Children by Means of a Group-Scale of Intelligence." They examined 187 colored and 2,800 white children of the same ages and drawn from the schools of the same area. They conclude: "The colored children of a given age average at about the average for white children (in the same city) two years younger"; and they add: "Analysis by test shows the colored children to

Haiti and Liberia. It is not in the least invalidated by the statistics we so often see, showing the progress of the colored people since emancipation, and by the acknowledged fact that some men of color have shown themselves to be truly great men.[1]

Now let us turn to a second question. These differences of intellectual capacity are inborn; but are they hereditary? We have already noted certain facts which imply the positive answer. If the differences are racial, they are hereditary in the race. But within the same race, or in a population blended from many closely allied stocks, such as the white Americans, are they hereditary?

---

average below white children of the same age on all the tests." This difference between white and colored children is the more significant, if we take into account the view which is widely held and which is probably true of many if not of all cases, namely, that inequality of adult intelligence is due, not so much to more rapid development of the more intelligent throughout childhood, but rather to an earlier arrest of development in the less intelligent.

[1] Shaler, who made a lifelong study of the Negroes and who wrote with warm appreciation of their many fine qualities, recorded, nevertheless, the following judgment: "All the facts we have point to the same unhappy conclusion, that the Negro considered as a species is, by nature, incapable of creating or maintaining societies of an

Well, we have seen that the lower levels, the levels of the mental defectives, are hereditary. Further, medical men have shown certain other forms of "mental defect" to be hereditary, *e. g.*, certain forms of insanity, or rather the predisposition to these, also the predisposition to epilepsy and the neuroses.

At the other end, the upper end of the scale, the studies of Galton[1] and his disciples have shown good ground for believing that exceptionally high intellectual capacity is hereditary. Standing alone, Galton's reasoning is perhaps inconclusive; and many have sought to escape his conclusions by attributing the achievements of the sons and grandsons of great men to their su-

---

order above barbarism, and that, so far as we can discern, this feature of his nature, depending, as it does, on the lack of certain qualities of mind, is irremediable" ("The Neighbor," p. 139). Again he wrote: "Unlike the most of the people who come to us from Europe, his race [the Negro] is not provided with the motives that lead to safety. His elevation and maintenance, so far as we can see for all time, absolutely depend upon the help he is to receive from the state-building race" (*op. cit.*, p. 172). It is thus apparent that the results of the recent application of the exacter methods of mental measurement bear out the opinion of impartial judges based upon long and careful observation of the less exact kind.

[1] "Hereditary Genius."

perior opportunities. But, when taken with the rest of the evidence, Galton's conclusions seem to me to be in the main incontestable, for they are in line with and harmonize with all the rest.

If, then, the degrees of intellectual capacity at the extremes of the scale are hereditary, it seems highly probable that the same is true of the intermediate part of the scale. But have we any direct evidence of this? Is there any evidence that the intellectual capacity of the ordinary plain citizen, of you and me and Smith and Jones, is determined largely by heredity? Common observation seems to point that way, but it is inconclusive. And we have hitherto only the beginnings of a direct attack on this problem. Professor K. Pearson[1] has produced some evidence that mental qualities are transmissible in exactly the same degree as physical qualities. He is a great statistician, but the mental qualities he dealt with are vague ill-defined conceptions, and his conclusions are open to criticism on that ground. Some years before the war one of my pupils at Oxford made a direct attack on the problem, and the results are significant, though on a small scale. At Oxford are gathered as

---

[1] Biometrika, vol. III.

teachers many men from the whole British Empire, highly selected in virtue of intellectual distinction. Now it so happens that in a certain private school in Oxford a majority of the boys are sons of these men. We therefore set out to compare the intellectual capacity of the boys of this school with that of boys of another school corresponding to your public schools. This "public school"[1] was an exceptionally good school of its kind, the teaching being in many respects better than in the other—the private school; the boys were from good homes, sons of good plain citizens—shopkeepers and skilled artisans, and so forth.

Without going into detail I may say summarily that the result was to show a very marked superiority of the boys of the school frequented by the intellectual class.[2] The result is all the

---

[1] In the American sense of the term.

[2] Mr. H. B. English, who conducted this research, has reported it in the *Yale Psychological Studies* for 1917: "Mental Capacity of School Children Correlated with Social Status." Mr. English concludes: "Although the groups are small, they are exceedingly homogeneous and thoroughly representative of the children in two social or economic strata. The writer does not hesitate, therefore, to predicate these results for the children of the entire classes represented or to conclude that the children of

more striking, if you reflect on the following facts: First, every boy has two parents and inherits his qualities from both. Secondly, it has not been shown that university dons prefer clever wives, or that they are particularly clever in choosing clever wives. There is room for difference of opinion. It remains, then, highly probable that, if the wives of these men were all as superior in respect of intellect as their husbands, the superiority of their sons to the boys of the other group would have been still more marked.

The result suggests a question of very great interest. Does the social stratification of society correspond to, is it correlated with, a stratification of intellectual capacity? The positive answer has been widely assumed on general grounds of probability by those who have studied heredity. Others ridicule the idea, and produce, as usual, their instances which do not conform to any such general rule. The result of the research just now mentioned supports the positive answer.

---

the professional class exhibit between 12 and 14 years of age a very marked superiority in intelligence." "Although he is not prepared to say, and does not in fact believe, that environment has had nothing to do with the superiority of one group over the other, he is convinced that *the hereditary factor plays an altogether predominant part.*"

But the question is extremely important, and I cite therefore the results of another direct attack on the problem.[1] Miss A. H. Arlitt (of Bryn Mawr College) tested 342 children from the primary grades of schools of one district. Of these, 191 were of American-born white parents, 80 were born of Italian immigrants, 71 were colored. They all spoke English without difficulty. The Americans were divided, according to the social status of their parents, into five groups, corresponding to those defined by Professor Taussig: (1) professional; (2) semi-professional and higher business; (3) skilled labor; (4) semi-skilled labor; and (5) unskilled labor. Groups (4) and (5) were amalgamated.

The results show very marked differences between the groups. They give four dissimilar curves of distribution. The medians (I. Q.) of the four groups were (1) 125, (2) 118, (3) 107, (4) 92.

[1] I may cite also similar results obtained by another of my pupils at Oxford, Mr. Cyril Burt, who concludes his article as follows: "For all these reasons we may conclude that the superior proficiency at intelligence-tests on the part of the boys of superior parentage was inborn. And thus we seem to have proved marked inheritability in the case of a mental character of the highest 'civic worth.'" "Experimental Tests of General Intelligence," *British Journal of Psychology*, vol. III, 1909.

I. Q. stands for "intelligence quotient," and is commonly used as a convenient abbreviation for "intellectual capacity as revealed by mental testing." The "median" is considered to be a rather more satisfactory figure than "the average" for the comparison of one group with another; it is commonly not widely different from "the average." The following table expresses the grades of intelligence attributed to the various groups on the basis of the testing.

TABLE IV

Americans of social status (1)				I. Q.	=	125
" " " " (2)				I. Q.	=	118
" " " " (3)				I. Q.	=	107
" " " " (4)				I. Q.	=	92
Italians				I. Q.	=	84[1]
Colored				I. Q.	=	83
All Americans grouped together				I. Q.	=	106

[1] If this figure should be confirmed by further research, it would, of course, not justify us in drawing any inference about the population of Italy as a whole, nor even about that of Southern Italy, from which region most of these immigrants have probably come. The recent Italian immigrants are probably not a fair sample of the population of Italy. I have omitted the decimal figures from Miss Arlitt's figures. I am much indebted to her for sending me details of her observations. Her full paper has not yet been published (summary in *Psychological Bulletin*, February, 1921).

It is noteworthy that Professor Terman, a high author-

A third research of a similar kind points to the same conclusion.[1] Tests were made of 548 children from the schools of one city. The children were arranged in four groups according to the occupation of their father, namely professional, executive, artisan, labor. The results are stated in terms of the percentage of children of each group who scored a mark higher than the median mark for the whole number of 548 children, and are as follows:—professional group, 85 per cent; executive group, 68 per cent; artisan group, 41 per cent; labor group, 39 per cent.[2]

---

ity, has found similar indications in working with the children of Italian and Spanish and Portuguese immigrants. In his book ("Intelligence of School Children," New York, 1919, p. 56) he gives the following figures for the I. Q., or measure of relative intelligence of the following classes of children drawn from the same schools:

Spanish...............................	78
Portuguese............................	84
Italian...............................	84
North European.......................	105
American.............................	106

[1] S. L. Pressey and R. Ralston, *Journal of Applied Psychology*, vol. III, 1919: "The Relation of General Intelligence of School Children to Occupation of the Father."

[2] Professor Terman, reporting on the results of tests applied to a large number of American school-children, states:

We have, then, pretty good evidence that capacity for intellectual growth is inborn in different degrees, that it is hereditary, and also that

---

"Intelligence of 110 to 120 I. Q. [this range is defined as 'superior intelligence,' the bulk of the children, about 60 per cent, ranging from 90 to 110 I. Q.] is approximately five times as common among children of superior social status as among children of inferior social status, the proportion among the former being about 24 per cent of all and among the latter only 5 per cent of all. The group [i. e., the group of 'superior intelligence'] is made up largely of children of the fairly successful mercantile or professional classes." He defines as of "very superior intelligence" those children who scored in the tests more than 120 marks. "Children of this group are . . . unusually superior. Not more than 3 out of 100 (i. e., of all tested) go as high as 125 I. Q., and only about 1 out of 100 as high as 130. In the schools of a city of average population only about 1 child in 250 or 300 tests as high as 140 I. Q. In a series of 476 unselected children there was not a single one reaching 120 whose social class was described as 'below average.' Of the children of superior social status, about 10 per cent reached 120 or better. The 120–140 group (i. e., of very superior intelligence) is made up almost entirely of children whose parents belong to the professional or very successful business classes. The child of a skilled laborer belongs here occasionally, the child of a common laborer very rarely indeed. At least this is true in the smaller cities of California among populations made up of native-born Americans." ("The Measurement of Intelligence," p. 95, New York, 1916.)

it is closely correlated with social status.[1] Further, we have good evidence that different races possess it in widely different degrees; that races differ in intellectual stature, just as they differ in physical stature.

We have considered so far only one human quality, intellectual capacity. This is very important. But other qualities also are important. We know how a man or a boy of normal, or superior, intellectual capacity may fail to make good for lack of moral qualities. We know that the moral qualities show a considerable independence of intellectual capacity. In regard to them the same questions arise. Are they inborn in various degrees? Are they hereditary? Are they distributed in different degrees and combinations in races and in the strata of the population of such a country as this?

These questions are even more difficult, and more apt to provoke acute differences of opinion, than the similar questions regarding intellectual capacity. Experimental psychology has hardly

---

[1] It seems highly probable that degrees of intelligence are not merely correlated with degrees of social status, but that intelligence is related to social status as ground to consequent or cause to effect. For yet another piece of evidence supporting this all-important conclusion, see p. 152.

begun to contemplate these problems; we have to glean our evidence from other sources. One small piece obtained by the experimental method seems worth citing as a suggestion. Mr. K. T. Waugh applied a number of tests to students in four colleges of British India (Lucknow), one Chinese college, and some American colleges. The tests were largely concerned with memory, and were not well suited to test intellectual capacity. They revealed only slight differences, which were slightly in favor of the Indian students—except in one quality, namely power of concentrating the attention.[1] In this the Chinese exactly equalled

---

[1] Mr. Waugh's report was made to the meeting of the American Psychological Association at Chicago, December, 1920 ("Comparison of Oriental and American Student Intelligence"). The functions tested were (1) concentration of attention, (2) speed of learning, (3) association-time, (4) immediate memory, (5) deferred memory, (6) range of information. His results are embodied in the following table:

TEST	SCORES		
	AMERICAN	CHINESE	INDIAN
1	75	75	62
2	66	62	45
3	46	38	58
4	58	..	54
5	80	..	88
6	23	15	24

the Americans; the Indians fell decidedly short
of them.   The facts that in other tests the Indians
equalled or excelled the Americans, and that in
two tests, which measure the power of concentration of attention, the Chinese equalled, while the
Indians fell far short of the Americans—these
facts inspire confidence in the objectivity of this
result.   They go far to show that the differences
found are not due to racial bias in favor of his
own race on the part of the observer, or to conditions of experimenting unduly favorable to the
American students.   This result seems to me
extraordinarily interesting and suggestive.   For
what is this power of concentrating attention?
It is essentially will-power.   I need only remind
you of what William James wrote of this.[1]   Now
the more or less orderly and successful government of the three hundred millions of India by a
mere handful of British men, during more than a

Where retentiveness is equal but speed of learning unequal, and power of concentration correlated with superior
speed of learning, we may safely attribute the superiority
in speed to superiority of concentration.

[1] "Effort of attention is thus the essential phenomenon
of will" ("Principles of Psychology," vol. II, p. 562).
Compare also the discussion and similar conclusion on this
topic in Doctor Maxwell Garnett's "Education and World-
Citizenship."

century, is one of the most remarkable facts in the history of the world. It is a marvellous achievement. And Englishmen have marvelled over it. And, when they have sought to explain how it has been possible, they have always come to the same conclusion. They have recognized that the natives of India, or very many of them, have much intellectual capacity; that they are clever, quick, versatile, retentive; that some of them have brilliant intellects. But such observers have frequently expressed the opinion that, as compared with their British rulers, the natives of India are relatively defective in character or will-power; and they have found the explanation of British ascendancy in this fact. Now, at the very first attempt to apply exact methods in the comparative study of Indians, this opinion finds confirmation. If this conclusion is really well-founded, as it seems to be, might we not infer from it that, if the qualities of Indians and British had been reversed in this single respect—if the Indians had been as innately superior in will-power as they seem to be inferior —then, not improbably, a few Indians would at the present time be ruling over and administering the affairs of all Europe, and perhaps of all America as well? It is a strange reflection. It is not utterly fantastic and absurd. It may at least serve to suggest how profoundly peculiarities of moral constitution may affect the destinies of peoples.

In this connection let me remind you that the quelling of the Indian Mutiny was, before all things, a triumph of will-power. If even a few of the British leaders, if Havelock, John Nicholson, and Baird Smith, and one or two others had failed, ever so little, in the supreme tests of will-power from which they came out triumphant, the British would have been swept from the country, and British rule in India would have been brought to an end about the year 1857.

IV

THE moral factors of human nature are very complex. Let us turn to the field of art, and see whether we cannot find in the arts of Europe the expression of racial peculiarities of moral constitution. The problem of racial manifestations in Europe would be simpler if we could assume, as has sometimes been done, that the population of Europe, or of western Europe, represents in the main two distinct races, the so-called Latin and Teutonic races. But anthropologists are pretty well agreed that it is derived in the main from three distinct races, which, although much mixed and partially blended in all countries, are spread out in three great east-to-west bands; the tall fair Nordic race in the North; the short dark long-headed Mediterranean race in the South; the darkish round-headed Alpine race in between; that is to say, the blood of each of these races predominates in these three zones respectively. In spite of this complication, we may contrast the art of the South with that of the North, and inquire how far any constant and general differences are attributable to differences of racial composition or anthropologic constitution.

Mr. A. Gehring[1] has drawn such a contrast most skilfully; and, lest I should seem to be affected by any bias of my own, I will follow his lead closely, attempting to give you the pith of his observations.

He contrasts the art of the Nordic race with that of the Græco-Latins in whom the blood of the Mediterranean race predominates. Taking one art after another, he shows that the same essential differences appear. In all arts the classic qualities predominate in the South, the romantic in the North.

The classic qualities are clearness, formality, circumscription, simplicity, directness of appeal to the senses, elegance, symmetry, proportion, observance of the unities of time and place, rationalism, and, I think we may add, a high degree of a quality only recently pointed out as a fundamental quality of works of art, namely the preservation of what is called "psychical distance"; that is to say, the subject, the topic, is kept remote, more or less unreal, and subordinate, while the essential of success lies in the form of the artist's treatment.[2]

---

[1] "Racial Contrasts," 1908.
[2] *Cf.* "The Æsthetic Attitude," by H. S. Langfeld, 1920.

The romantic qualities are the opposite of these—profusion of characters, of qualities, situations, objects and details, and of suggestions of all these things beyond those actually portrayed or presented; complexity of relations, of plot, of design, of emotions; indirectness of appeal, relying upon suggestion of a wealth of imagery and vague meaning, by the figurative and symbolical usage of all material; the suggestion of mystery, of the unknown and unfathomable; all prompting, not so much to direct and purely æsthetic enjoyment, as to moral and mystical reflection on man and nature.

To illustrate these differences I will only ask you to compare mentally: classical with northern mythology; a classical temple with a gothic cathedral; the best Italian painting with works of Rubens, Dürer, Turner, Rembrandt; Italian music with the music of Wagner and Beethoven; the classical theatre with the plays of Shakespeare and Goethe's Faust; Homer and Virgil and Horace with Wordsworth, Shelley, Carlyle, Coleridge, and Meredith. If we would see the contrast in its full degree, we must compare the greatest works of the greatest artists; for in these the inward nature of the artist is most truly and spontaneously expressed. There are no doubt exceptions (*e. g.*, Michael Angelo and Dante[1]), but on the whole the contrast is striking and of the same nature in all the arts. Other writers have pointed out the same differences, and some have suggested explanations. M. Boutmy, for example, would attribute the difference to the influence of climate: the mystical, reflective, introspective quality of Northern art to the foggy atmosphere; the clear, direct appeal to the senses in the South to the clear sunny atmosphere.[2] This is hardly an adequate explanation. For we see that, when a predominantly Nordic people, such as the English, transfers itself to another climate, to New England, where it enjoys a latitude and a brilliant climate comparable to those of southern Europe, it continues in its art to exhibit the same peculiarities; they are nowhere more strongly presented than in the works of Emerson and Whitman and of other American writers. If climate has anything to do with the production of the difference, the effects of climate

---

[1] It must be remembered that there was a strong infusion of Nordic blood in northern Italy; and, though it seems to have left few physical traces at the present time, it was probably more strongly represented at the time of the Renaissance than it is now.

[2] "La psychologie du peuple anglais."

must have become impressed on the mind, transmissible and hereditary, through many generations of influence.

Mr. Gehring discerningly remarks: "It is con-
ceivable that vast differences in national activities and institutions are the results of insignificant divergences of mental structure." This is,
I think, very true, if we insert the word *seemingly*
before "insignificant divergences of mental structure." Is it possible to point to any divergence
of mental structure between the Mediterranean
and the Nordic races which would explain wholly
or in part these wide differences of expression in
art? What constitutional innate differences do
these express? And can we find other differences
of activity which seem to express the same divergence of mental structure or moral endowment?
In seeking such innate differences we may properly
turn to the instinctive endowment. We have
recently come to recognize, thanks chiefly to
William James, that human nature comprises a
number of distinct instinctive tendencies or instincts; that these, though deeply hidden and
disguised in the adult man, are nevertheless the
mainsprings of all our activities, bodily, emotional, and intellectual; that one man differs
from another in the native strength of these sev-

eral instincts.[1] And, though it seems clear that the same instincts are common to the whole human species, it may be that one race differs from another (statistically) in respect of the relative strengths of the several instincts.

In seeking an explanation along this line, we must not postulate a special instinct as the underlying ground of every special form of national activity, as the literary historians too often have done.[2] We may only invoke, for our historical explanations, instincts which on other grounds we have found reason to believe to be common to the whole human race, and which conform to the psychological and biological conception of instinct.

Let us notice first how some great critics have endeavored to define the essence of the romantic quality in art. Walter Pater said: "It is the

---

[1] *Cf.* my "Introduction to Social Psychology," where the part of instincts in human life is discussed at length.

[2] Renan was the great exponent of this *ad hoc* invention of instincts, this facile mode of explanation of historical facts; *e. g.*, in his polemic against the Jews, he asserted that they were devoid of the instincts for mythology, for polytheism, for epic, for drama, for politics, and for military organization. He never stopped to inquire whether any people possess such instincts, nor even to ask what he meant by the word "instinct."

addition of strangeness to beauty that constitutes
the romantic character in art; and the desire of
beauty being a fixed element in every artistic
organization, it is the addition of *curiosity* to
this desire of beauty that constitutes the romantic
temper." Another critic gives substantially the
same definition of the romantic. "If we analyze
the feeling we shall find, I think, that it has its
origin in wonder and mystery. It is the sense
of something hidden, of imperfect revelation."
(Hedge.)

Curiosity or wonder, then, seems to be the
essence of the romantic. Now, curiosity, with the
emotion of wonder which enters as an essential
element into all such emotions as awe, admiration,
and reverence, seems to be due to the working
within us of a true primitive instinct.[1] If we
assume that this instinct is stronger in the Nordic
than in the Mediterranean race, we shall have
an hypothesis which will partly explain the difference between their arts; namely, it will largely
explain the romantic quality of Northern art.
Is there any other difference which fits this assumption? Well, curiosity or wonder may, with-

---

[1] *Cf.* my "Social Psychology," pp. 57, 129, and chapter
XIII.

out exaggeration, be called the mother of philosophy and of science. Now modern science is
very largely a product of northern Europe, of
those countries where the Nordic blood predominates; not exclusively so by any means. But
note this fact: the Greeks, who founded philosophy and science, were probably, in their great
age, compounded of the Nordic and the Mediterranean races. The Romans were almost purely
Mediterranean. They produced great men, great
lawyers, soldiers, administrators, and poets; but
no philosophy and no science. For four hundred
years they ruled absolutely the fairest part of
the world, in a state of high civilization; but
they invented nothing, discovered nothing, made
no progress in science. Otto Seeck, the historian
of the decay of the classical world, has drawn a
vivid picture of this scientific stagnation.[1] He
points out how even in the art of war, on success in which their whole empire was founded
and maintained, the Romans made no progress,
invented no new weapons, but fought in the same
old way with the same old weapons throughout
the centuries of their predominance. Note another indication of the weakness of their curiosity.

---

[1] "Geschichte des Untergangs der antiken Welt."

In spite of their supremacy, their high civilization, their navy and mercantile marine, they
remained a Mediterranean power: their sailors
penetrated hardly, if at all, beyond the pillars
of Hercules; while the barbarous Vikings in their
smaller ships sailed to Iceland, Greenland, and
America, and perhaps landed on the banks of
the Charles River. Here, then, is further evidence that in the Mediterranean race the instinct
of curiosity is relatively weak. But wonder, if it
is the mother of science, is also an essential element in religion, entering, as I said, into the
religious emotions of awe, admiration, and reverence. It follows that, if our hypothesis is correct,
we should expect to find some appreciable difference between the religions of Northern and
Southern Europe. To that topic I will return.[1]

Let us pursue further the differences revealed
in art. For the hypothesis of a stronger dose of
curiosity in the Nordic race will only partially
explain these differences. Are there indications
of a similar difference between the Mediterranean
and the Nordic races in respect of any other of

---

[1] My friend, Mr. Gilbertson, has drawn my attention
to the fact that in some of the Norse folk-tales the younger
brother triumphs over his scornful elders by reason of his
insatiable curiosity. A very significant fact.

the human instincts? I seem to see clear indications of one other such difference. The Southern
Europeans are more sociable than the Northern.
They delight in conversation, in coming together
in large masses, in expressing their emotions collectively, in great collective outbursts of applause,
of admiration, or of execration. In all ages their
civilization has been essentially an urban civilization; they are naturally urbane; the city has
always been their natural habitat.

Men of Nordic race, on the other hand, are
taciturn; they take part in social gatherings only
with difficulty and hesitation; they are content
to live alone in the seclusion of the family circle,
emerging from it only in response to the call of
duty or ambition or war. The isolated home is
their invention, their dearest possession; and the
individualized family home is one of their peculiar
contributions to the culture of the world.[1] The
facts are all summed up in the phrase—"An Eng-
lishman's home is his castle." This difference
runs through every form and detail of social life
and organization. We may safely infer that it
is the expression of an innate difference of constitution.

---

[1] Cf. "Histoire de la formation particulariste," by Henri
de Tourville, Paris, 1905.

What is it, then, that impels men to gather together without ulterior purpose, to shrink from isolation as the most intolerable of evils, to find satisfaction in merely being together *en masse?* It is the working of a distinct and now generally recognized instinct, common to the human species and all the gregarious mammals; it is the impulse of the gregarious or herd instinct. We have, it seems, good reason to add to our hypothesis the assumption that this herd instinct is relatively weak in the Nordic, strong in the Mediterranean, peoples. We now have a fuller explanation of the differences between the arts of the two peoples. The art of the Mediterraneans is essentially and most characteristically public art, the art of the theatre, of the orator, sculpture, architecture, and poetry for public recitation at festivals; and worship is essentially a public, formal, ritualistic act. Their art is, in all its forms, markedly objective and conventional; and "conventional" means that it observes generally recognized rules which render it easily intelligible to the masses.

The art of the North, on the other hand, is subjective, individual, peculiar, defying or ignoring all conventions. And the arts most characteristic of the North are reflective nature poetry and the novel or romance which reflectively portrays and analyzes character; both, you see, forms of art fit to be enjoyed only in isolation, by the brooding reader who is content to be moved to laughter or to tears in solitude.

The Nordic race, then, is more curious and less sociable than the Mediterranean. In it the instinct of curiosity is stronger, the herd instinct is weaker. But still we do not seem to have an hypothesis capable of explaining fully the divergences of Northern from Southern art. The vividness and directness of appeal of Southern art, its more passionate, more sensuous quality, still require explanation. These qualities we may naturally associate with a universally recognized difference between the peoples who have created these arts. The Mediterranean peoples are vivacious, quick, impetuous, impulsive; their emotions blaze out vividly and instantaneously into violent expression and violent action. The Northern peoples are slow, reserved, unexpressive; their emotions seem to escape in bodily expression and action with difficulty. If we recognize this as a constitutional difference between the Mediterranean and the Nordic races, we complete the hypothesis needed for the explanation of their divergences in art.

But can we form any valid conception of such

a constitutional difference? It is sometimes assumed that in the Southern peoples the emotions and their impulses are inherently stronger than in the Northern. This seems to me entirely fallacious. If it were true, we should except to find the Northern peoples comparatively inert, placid, sluggish, inactive. But see what they have done: their restless energy is chiefly responsible for the transformation of the modern world; they primarily have peopled North America and Australia, governed India, penetrated to the heart of Africa, settled in every island of Malaysia and the Pacific Ocean, scaled almost all the great mountains and reached the North and the South Poles.

It is obvious that no difference in the relative strength of any instinct could account for the difference we are now considering; for the difference finds expression in all emotions and in all modes of activity. It seems to be a perfectly general difference of constitution; whereas all instincts are more or less specific.

Well, modern medicine comes to our help and suggests the true explanation. The modern psychological study of the so-called nervous disorders has shown that the functional nervous disorders are really of mental origin, and that they fall into two distinct groups, of which hysteria and neurasthenia are the types, respectively. Now it is found that men and women who break down under nervous strain or emotional shocks tend to develop symptoms of the one or other kind, according as they belong to one or other of two constitutional types. We owe the clear distinction of these two types to Doctor C. G. Jung of Zurich.[1] He calls them the extrovert and the introvert types. The well-marked extroverts are those whose emotions flow out easily into bodily expression and action. They are the vivid, vivacious, active persons who charm us by their ease and freedom of expression, their frankness, their quick sympathetic responses. They are little given to introspective brooding; they remain relatively ignorant of themselves; for they are essentially objective, they are interested directly and primarily in the outer world about them. When and if they break down under strain, their trouble takes on the hysteric type, the form of dissociations, paralyses, anesthesias, amnesias; in spite of which they may remain cheerful, active, and interested in the world.

The introvert, on the other hand, is slow and reserved in the expression of his emotions. He has difficulty in adequately expressing himself.

[1] "Analytic Psychology."

His nervous and mental energies, instead of flowing out freely to meet and play upon the outer world, seem apt to turn inward, determining him to brooding, reflection, deliberation before action. And, when he is subject to strain, his energies are absorbed in internal conflicts; he becomes dead to the outer world, languid, absorbed, self-centred, and full of vague distress.

Now, this difference of constitutional type is not due to difference of environment and training. Within the same family you may see well-marked examples of both types, though all have been subjected to almost identical environmental influences. The difference between the two types seems to be the expression of a subtle difference of physiological constitution which pervades every part of the nervous system. What exactly it consists in we do not know. Many years ago I threw out an hypothesis as to the nature of this peculiarity of nervous constitution and I believe it is essentially correct or on the right lines. But it is too technical a matter to discuss here. Suffice it to say that it seems to explain the facts, and the suggested peculiarity is one which may well be transmitted hereditarily.[1]

[1] "The Conditions of Fatigue in the Nervous System," *Brain*, vol. XXXII, 1909.

Now, physicians who have specialized in nervous disorders in both the North and South of Europe assure me that the Northerners are much more commonly subject to the neurasthenic type of trouble, the Southerners to the hysteric type. This fits exactly with the universally recognized difference between North and South.

We may fairly complete our hypothesis by assuming that the Mediterranean race is constitutionally extrovert, the Nordic race constitutionally introvert. Of course, exceptions may occur; the statement can be only statistically true; and especially, in view of the fact of the wide mixture of blood of the two races, and the peculiar mixture of innate qualities that results from race blending, we may expect many mixed and ill-defined types; which is what we actually find.

We seem now to have completed our hypothesis for the explanation of the divergence of the North from the South of Europe in respect of their artistic expressions. The Nordic race is constitutionally introvert; it is strong in the instinct of curiosity, the root of wonder; weak in the herd instinct, the root of sociability. In the Mediterranean race these peculiarities are reversed; it is extrovert, weak in curiosity, strong in sociability.

If our hypothesis is correct we should expect to find other differences between North and South to the explanation of which it may be applied.[1] In discussing art it was possible to leave out of our view the third great race which has contributed a full share of its blood to the population of modern Europe, namely the Alpine race, which geographically occupies, or predominates in, the middle zone. For the art of this race (the art of the Slavs, and that generally known as Celtic) has been somewhat apart from the two great rival traditions, the classical and the romantic. But at this point we must bring this race into our

---

[1] One such striking difference, which may be noted in passing, is the greater proneness to alcoholic intoxication of the Nordic peoples and the great sobriety in this respect of the Mediterranean peoples. Sir Archdall Reid (in his "Present Evolution of Man") has argued that the greater sobriety of the populations of the South of Europe is the consequence of their longer usage of alcoholic liquors, which he supposes to have weeded out from them all strains peculiarly susceptible to their influence. It seems to me more probable that the explanation is to be found in the introvert quality of the Nordic race. Alcohol acts on the nervous system in a way which renders it temporarily extrovert; and thus for the introvert it brings relief from the brooding melancholy to which he is constitutionally liable; it enables him to enjoy the freedom of emotional expression which in his normal condition is denied him by his introvert constitution.

discussion. It must suffice to say that, in both physical and mental qualities, it seems to stand between the Mediterranean and the Nordic races. Physically it is distinguished from the Mediterranean race by having a round rather than a long head. Mentally, it seems to be introvert rather than extrovert, but not so extremely introvert as the Nordic race. It has in common with the Mediterranean race a high degree of sociability; and is, I think, though here I speak less confidently, like it, relatively weak in curiosity.

The Nordic race is, then, to be distinguished physically from the other two races by fair hair and complexion and by high stature. And it seems to be unlike both of them in respect of the three mental qualities we have defined. These two physical qualities serve as the indicators of the blood of this race; and maps of the physical qualities of the European peoples show clearly the regions of its predominance. Are there any maps revealing a similar distribution of mental or moral peculiarities? I will put before you some maps which show the distribution of certain physical and moral traits.

The first map shows that fair complexion predominates in the northeastern part of France, and that this area of "fairness" is prolonged in two

BRUNETNESS
FRANCE

RELATIVE
ORDER
OF
DEPARTMENTS

W.Z.R.

AFTER TOPINARD
200,000 OBSERVATIONS

directions, namely southwestward to Bordeaux and southward along the valley of the Rhone. The map of the distribution of stature agrees closely with this, showing predominance of tall stature in the same regions.[1] Historical and archæological evidence shows that these are the regions in which the Nordic tribes established

---

[1] *Cf.* Professor Z. Ripley's "Races of Europe." I am indebted to Professor Ripley for his permission to reproduce these maps.

INTENSITY OF SUICIDE
FRANCE
1872-6
After MORSELLI '82

PER
MILLION
INHABITANTS.

Under 50
51-75
76-100
101-150
151-200
201-250
250-300
Above 350

themselves most fully, driving out or extermi-
nating in large measure their forerunners of Alpine and Mediterranean race.

Now examine the map showing the relative frequency of suicide in the provinces of modern
France. You see that this map corresponds very
closely with the other. Wherever the physical
marks (fair complexion and high stature) of the
Nordic race predominate, there suicide is frequent,
and conversely.

The suggestion is that suicide is frequent in proportion to the predominance of Nordic blood. E. Morselli (the Italian alienist) has pointed out this correlation and has deduced the conclusion that the Nordic race is more apt at suicide than the other European races. Cautious anthropologists (including Professor Ripley, from whose valuable book on "The Races of Europe" I have copied these maps) have refused to follow him. It is necessary to be something of a psychologist, perhaps, if one is to appreciate the evidence. For other men of science, even the medical men, are systematically trained to ignore the mind of man. For them it is something unreal, because intangible. They are willing to attribute such a phenomenon as the prevalence of suicide in an area to climate, or diet, or geological formation, or the electric disturbances of the atmosphere, for all these are "real." But to attribute it to mental peculiarities or conditions seems to them pure mythology.

Well, Morselli traced and mapped the frequency of suicide in all parts of Europe. It must be admitted that he relied too much upon language as a criterion of race; and he showed very convincingly that there is a very high correlation between suicide and the use of the German language, that

those who speak German are very apt to commit
suicide. Some of you may at once infer that the
language is the cause of the suicide; and perhaps
it would be difficult completely to refute such a
simple and attractive theory. But, looking at
the facts more widely, we see that the frequency
of suicide is correlated not only, or chiefly, with
language, but rather with the physical qualities of
the Nordic race. Take France; the correlation is
close. Professor Ripley suggests it is due to the
fact that the Nordics occupy the regions of greatest industrial activity and prosperity, where larger
towns are frequent. But that they occupy these
regions is a fact which in turn requires explanation. Turn, then, to another detailed map—that
of England.

Notice that there are three regions in which
suicide is least frequent, namely Wales, Cornwall, and an area lying a little to the north of
London. All three are areas in which the Nordic
blood is but little represented. The Welsh represent the pre-Saxon population, with little admix-
ture of Nordic blood; and that they are mentally
very different from the English is a fact of common knowledge. Very striking is the contrast
between Cornwall and Devonshire. Every sum-
mer visitor to these counties notices the very

marked mental differences between their populations. Devonshire is a typically English county. Its population has played a prominent part in many of the most characteristically English activities, especially in sea-roving, in colonial adventure, and pioneering. It is the traditional home of the English "sea-kings." The population of Cornwall, like that of Wales, is in the main descended from the British tribes which were driven westward by the Anglo-Saxon invaders. Among them the ancient British language has only recently died out. In respect of all other conditions, the two counties are extremely similar, save that Devonshire is rather more fertile. Both are predominantly agricultural and pastoral and seafaring, with an equable mild climate. Yet, as regards the frequency of suicide, we see the large difference indicated by the map. Perhaps even more striking is the small area north of London. The physical anthropologists have shown that, owing to circumstances not fully understood, the population of this region shows predominance of the physical qualities of the pre-English or British tribes. It seems to be an island of the old British population, surrounded by, but not displaced or swamped by, the tide of Anglo-Saxon invasion. And in this small island of population, the physical and economic conditions of which differ hardly appreciably from those of the surrounding counties, suicide remains at its lowest rate, namely that of Wales and Cornwall.

On the other hand, suicide reaches its highest rate in Sussex, the population of which county is perhaps the most purely and typically Saxon of all England.

Now consider Table V.

TABLE V

ANNUAL SUICIDES PER MILLION POPULATION[1]

Denmark	268
Scandinavia	127
N. Germany	150
S. Germany	165
England	72
S. Australia	90
Wales	52
Ireland	10
Spain	17
Russia	30
N. Italy	46
S. Italy	26

It will be seen that suicide is most frequent in the Scandinavian countries, those of which the population is most purely Nordic; moderately high in England and South Australia, where the population shows a fair proportion of the physical qualities of the Nordic race. The rate is very low in Ireland, in spite of all the political troubles and economic distress of her people; and very low in Spain, South Italy, and Russia, where the Nordic blood is scarce.

In view of all these facts, we can hardly doubt that the racial hypothesis contains much truth. Of course, other factors than race are important.

---

[1] This table is extracted from E. Morselli's "Le Suicide."

Germany, north and south, has undue pre-eminence; it may be due to language or government or other lack of harmony. But the facts, taken all together, do strongly support the racial hypothesis. And they do so the more strongly, if we take into consideration the following facts. Suicide is a form of violence, of homicide; we might, then, on superficial consideration, expect to find suicide most frequent where other forms of violence and of homicide abound. But the facts are just the converse of this expectation. It is in Southern Italy, Corsica, and Sardinia, where the population is most purely Mediterranean, that crimes of violence, especially homicide, are most frequent; while suicide is very infrequent. Further, suicide is three to four times as frequent among men as among women in all peoples. It is fourteen times as frequent among the whites of New York State as among the colored population, proportionately to their numbers. Can this be attributed to social advantages enjoyed by women all over the world, or by the colored people of New York? No; it is constitutional. The racial hypothesis is immensely strengthened, when we see that these peculiar features of the distribution of suicide and homicide are in perfect harmony with the conclusions we have drawn from the comparison of the arts of Northern and Southern Europe; they are just what we should expect, if the three European races differ in mental constitution in the ways assumed by our hypothesis.

But, before dwelling on this, let us glance at yet another moral peculiarity which still further strengthens the argument, namely the frequency of divorce. Maps of the frequency of divorce or separation in Europe show a close correlation of high frequency of divorce with the physical qualities of the Nordic race. The relation is disturbed by religious influences. But take France. We see that high frequency of divorce and separation occurs in the same areas in which suicide and the physical qualities of the Nordic race abound.

Well, the introvert and unsociable race is the one prone to suicide and divorce. The sociable and extrovert race is prone to homicide, but not to divorce or suicide. Is not this in accordance with the mental peculiarities which on other grounds we have assigned to the two races? We know that the introvert tends to brood over his difficulties; he readily becomes a prey to internal conflict of the emotions; and, as a matter of fact, such conflict does not only give rise to nervous disorder of the neurasthenic type, but, in not a few of these cases, leads on to suicide. As regards di-

FREQUENCY
DIVORCE
(SEPARATIONS)
FRANCE
1860 - 79
After J. BERTILLON '83

NORMANDIE

BRETAGNE

PER 1000
MARRIAGES

1 and 2
3 - 4
5 - 6
7 - 8
9 - 10
11 - 12
13 - 14
24
(PARIS)

LYON

SAVOIE

AUVERGNE

MARSEILLE

vorce, we may suppose that the injured Nordic, the unsociable introvert, broods over his wrongs, and then, nursing his resentment, either seeks redress in the law courts, or deserts his partner and becomes liable to be divorced for desertion. In the impulsive sociable extrovert, on the other hand, the emotion of anger blazes out, passes at once to action and often to homicide; and, when he is injured by the unfaithfulness of his partner, he does not brood upon the problem—he solves it

at once by using knife or pistol upon one or both
of the guilty parties.

Perhaps it is not fantastic to suppose that our
third point of difference also tends in the same
direction. The curious Nordic, we may suppose,
brooding and pondering in secret distress the
problem of his partner's infidelity, strives to understand how such an act has become possible:
while for the impetuous incurious Mediterranean
the fact alone suffices; his hand is not arrested by
any desire to understand the conditions which
have produced it.

And even in suicide curiosity may play its part.
Is not death a great adventure into the unknown?
May not the desire to know the last secret have
urged some reflective and unhappy souls, exas-
perated by the mystery of human life, to penetrate by their own act the impenetrable veil?

I will pass very quickly over another allied
topic, the distribution of the forms of religion.
The distribution of all the great religions of the
world presents interesting and suggestive questions of race, especially perhaps Buddhism, which,
after rising and spreading rapidly in India, passed
equally rapidly away eastward, to become endur-
ingly established among all branches of the yellow
race. But I will keep nearer home and insist

only on the distribution of Protestantism and of
Roman and Greek Catholicism, the three great
religious forms of Europe. The suggestion that
this is largely a matter of race is not new. It has
often been made and often denied. In the main
the two forms of Catholicism are religions of
authority, of convention, of ritual; they are pre-
eminently social in their rites and celebrations.
Only the Protestant reads his Bible in his closet
and communes alone with God, pondering the
problems of life and death. Only the Protestant
Church has split into a thousand peculiar sects,
each maintaining its peculiar creed and practice;
and only Protestants have traversed wide oceans
in search of lands where they might worship God
after their own fashion. Or, rather, Protestantism
is the only one of the three forms which permits
and even encourages such individualism and independence.

Now, of course, the vast majority of men grow
up in and adhere to the church of their fathers.
But the Protestants did, as a matter of historical
fact, break away from the Church of Rome; and
those who have broken away are in the main just
those peoples and those sections of nations in
which the physical qualities of the Nordic race
predominate; while all those in which the other

two races clearly predominate have remained subject to the Catholic Church of East or West.
Among the former are the populations of Northern France, Holland, Denmark, Scandinavia, Fin-
land, England, of most of Scotland, and of Northern Germany. Ireland, the western Highlands,
Southern France and Germany, and all to the
south and east of them remain subject to the
religions of authority. There are exceptions to
the rule, *e. g.*, Wales, Cornwall, parts of Belgium
and of Switzerland; and it is true that Calvin and
other great reformers belonged to Switzerland.
But other influences have played a part.

Is it, then, mere coincidence that the peoples in
which predominates the blood of the curious, in-
quiring, unsociable, reflective, introverted Nordic
race, and these only, with few small exceptions,
have broken away from the religions of authority,
of convention, of formal ritual, of outward action
and emotional display? The historian may point
to the personal and political circumstances of the
reign of Henry VIII of England, or suggest a
score of alternative explanations from the depths
of his learning. But he seems to me to ask too
much of our credulity, if he would ascribe the
whole correlation to a multitude of historical
accidents.

In this connection I would insist upon the importance of a principle which I have enunciated in my "Group Mind." [1] It is this. The innate mental qualities of any stably organized people or nation are revealed more clearly in the national character and in the national institutions than in the characters of individuals. For the character of each individual is very greatly moulded by the national institutions and traditions among which he grows up; to such an extent, in fact, that his native disposition may seem to be swamped, over-laid, and totally obscured by the tendencies acquired through training, imitation, and social pressure of all sorts. But the culture of each of the modern nations has been slowly built up, partly by original invention, but more largely by absorption of elements imitated from other nations. Of the family of nations, each contributes something to a common stock of culture derived by tradition from the past; from this common stock each nation selects what best suits its people; and, having adopted such an element, modifies it to suit its own nature more exactly. Thus the culture, the sum of the traditions and institutions, of each nation, grows in an environment which exerts constantly a selective and moulding influence upon it; just as, according to the Darwinian theory, the various species of animals have

---

[1] New York, 1920.

become slowly differentiated and evolved by the selective and moulding action of their environments. In the case of the national culture-species, the environment which thus selects and moulds the enduring elements is the sum of the native qualities of the people. I would call this *the law of the adaptation of the culture-species*. We may see illustrations of it on every hand. From the operation of this law it results that each nation which has enjoyed a long period of development, without serious interruption, has acquired traditions and institutions that are in harmony with its predominant native qualities. Therefore, in the development of each member of such a nation, nature and nurture work harmoniously together. Just for this reason it is so difficult to distinguish, in any one member of such a nation, the influence of his native disposition from that of the culture by which his development has been moulded.

This law is of little significance in relation to such peculiarities as the frequency of suicide and divorce. But it is of great importance in relation to all things regulated by legislation and by established custom and tradition, such things as religion and social organization, the form of the family, the village community, land-tenure, political and educational institutions.

Bearing this law in mind, let us examine what appears to be a particularly instructive instance of a large difference in the destinies of two peoples, determined by a small difference of anthropologic constitution.

I refer to the French and the British nations. Both stand in the van of Western civilization; both have produced many men of the first order in many spheres of activity. Each inhabits a beautiful, rich, and fertile country, of temperate climate, well placed geographically in every regard, cultural, climatic, commercial, military. In all these respects the French nation has, if anything, the advantage of the British.

Both nations have been great conquerors and colonists. Yet how different at the present time are their positions as world influences! The French have conquered and ruled immense areas of the surface of the earth. Yet nowhere outside France is there any large community of people of French descent and speech living under the French flag; nowhere save in Canada any considerable population of French descent.[1] And France's tenure of those great colonial territories

---

[1] It is said that approximately 1,000,000 of the population of the French possessions in North Africa are of French descent. This is to be set over against the millions of Australasia, Canada, and South Africa.

over which she now rules seems to be comparatively precarious and uncertain. Britain, on the other hand, not only administers the affairs of one-fifth of the people of the world, but has peopled North America and Australia, and keeps under her flag immense territories inhabited by her sons. And, while the French language and traditions seem to have small prospect of a future outside France, the English language and British traditions seem to be in a fair way to prevail increasingly throughout the world. Further, in nearly all her great colonial adventures—in India, in Canada, in Louisiana, in the West Indies, in China, in Africa—France has come into rivalry with the British and has been worsted.

Is all this great divergence of destiny due to a converging series of historical accidents? Or is there one underlying cause or condition? May we not fairly seek the ground of this difference of destiny in some difference of anthropologic constitution of the two nations? The key to the problem seems to me to have been given in a passage written long ago by a French traveller in this country, Volney. I will read you the passage in which he contrasts the French with the British colonist. "The French colonist deliberates with his wife upon everything that he proposes to do;

often the plans fall to the ground through lack
of agreement. . . . To visit one's neighbors, to
chat with them, is for the French an habitual
need so imperious that on all the frontier of
Louisiana and Canada you will not find a single
French colonist established beyond sight of his
neighbor's home. . . . On the other hand, the
English colonist, slow and taciturn, passes the
whole day continuously at work; at breakfast he
coldly gives his orders to his wife . . . and goes
forth to labor. If he finds an opportunity to sell
his farm at a profit, he does so and goes ten or
twenty leagues farther into the wilderness to make
himself a new home."

There you have, I suggest, the key to the difference we are examining. And this testimony does
not stand alone. It is in harmony with a great
number of social differences presented by the two
peoples; the centralized form of government in
France as against the local autonomies of Britain; the form of the French family and the laws
and customs regulating family life, e. g., the laws
of inheritance; the educational system as against
the English lack of educational system; the predominance of co-operative centrally organized
activities among the French; the individual enterprise and lack of systematic organization of the

British.[1] All these and other similar differences
have been pointed out and dwelt upon by many
French writers;[2] and various attempts have been
made to explain them as the result of historical
events, such as the more thorough Romanization
of Gaul, the conquest of England by William of
Normandy, the different operation of the feudal
system in the two countries. The English historian, T. H. Buckle, was one of those who dwelt
upon these differences and who claimed to explain them from such historical episodes. He
summed up the difference in two convenient
phrases, the predominance of the spirit of protection in France, and the predominance of the
spirit of independence in Britain. I will not delay to examine these proposed explanations and
to show you their inadequacy. I have done so
elsewhere.[3] I will only remark that so general

---

[1] The difference is strikingly illustrated by the Roman-
ized and codified law of France and the chaotic common
law of England, which is dominated by judge-made
precedents. I understand from Dean Roscoe Pound that
the law of England only narrowly escaped Romanization
at one period, thanks to the independent spirit of some
English lawyers.

[2] See especially Ed. Demolin's "A quoi tient la supé-
riorité des Anglo-Saxons?"

[3] "The Group Mind."

a phenomenon requires for its explanation a general deep-lying cause, such as is only to be found in some difference of native qualities between the two peoples.

Let us compare the two peoples in respect of racial composition as revealed by history and by physical anthropology. The French people seems to have been formed by a mixture and partial blending of the three great European races in approximately equal proportions. The British people seems to have been formed chiefly by a mixture and partial blending of the Nordic and the Mediterranean races; the Alpine, which probably predominates in France numerically, being hardly represented, and the Nordic predominating over the other elements. Probably most anthropologists would assign Nordic blood to Britain to the extent of 60 or 70 per cent, the rest being largely Mediterranean; and to France some 25 per cent Nordic blood, with perhaps 40 per cent Alpine and 35 per cent Mediterranean. This is a very rough estimate, of course.

We may ask: Given the moral peculiarities of the Nordic race which we have inferred on other grounds, does this considerably greater proportion of the blood and the qualities of that race suffice to account for the contrast between the two nations expressed by Buckle's phrase—the predominance of the spirit of protection in France and of the spirit of independence in Britain? It does, I think, go some way to explain it; especially if we note that sociability or gregariousness, which we saw to be strong in the Mediterranean race, is at least as strong, perhaps stronger, in the Alpines. We have seen from Volney's description how the sociability of the Frenchman handicaps him, as compared with the Briton, when he becomes a pioneer and colonist in new lands.

We may suppose also that the greater curiosity of the Nordic race contributes to give the Briton that restless wandering habit which has spread him over all the surface of the earth; so that, no matter to what remote region you may penetrate, you are apt to see some solitary Briton walk in on you and casually demand the loan of a copy of the London *Times*.

V

HAVING found reasons for assigning certain qualities to the three great races of Europe, we are attempting to apply this hypothesis to the explanation of that striking difference between the French and British nations which is summed up in the phrase—the prevalence in France of the spirit of protection, in Britain of the spirit of independence.

I said that the greater sociability of the French, which I attributed to the greater strength of the gregarious impulse in the Mediterranean and Alpine races, goes some way to explain this difference; and that the stronger curiosity of the Nordic race would also contribute to this difference.

But the differences between the institutions and customs of the two peoples at home and abroad seem to require the assumption of a further difference of innate quality. The Briton's intolerance of authority, his dislike of being controlled, governed, administered, and his preference for individual initiative, show themselves in all his conduct of affairs; they are well expressed in the accepted dictum that the British, when engaged in any large enterprise, "muddle through" somehow. They have always had to "muddle through," because they will not submit to being deliberately organized and led, according to any logically thought-out scheme. The first partial exception in their history was the acceptance of compulsory military service under the extreme pressure of the Great War.

The French, on the other hand, have always been ready to accept organization and leadership, to look for it to the State or to some man of dominating personality—a Napoleon, a Gambetta, a Boulanger, or a Richelieu.

We may note in passing that this tendency to seek personal leadership seems to be still stronger in the Germans, among whom the Alpine blood is even more strongly represented than in the French. Their docility under an autocratic and arbitrary bureaucracy; their suggestibility in all matters of belief; their devotion to the Kaiser (which even now threatens to restore him to the throne); the flourishing of a host of little princes and grand dukes; the spirit of caste, which leads each man to seek a definite position in the official hierarchy and from it to look up humbly to all above him in the scale—all these are significant of a society in which a docile race is dominated by one of a more self-assertive quality.[1] This actually and historically is, I suggest, the condition of affairs in Germany and the key to its history; and to a less degree it is true of France also.

The history of the purest stocks of the Nordic race illustrates abundantly and overwhelmingly their defect of docility, their possession in the highest degree of the opposite quality of self-

---

[1] The organization of Germany for her bid for world domination seems to have been in the main the work of the Prussian aristocracy, the Junkers, a class in which the Nordic blood preponderates. The tendency of the masses of the German people to proclaim "Deutschland über Alles" is a recent phenomenon, induced and sedulously cultivated in their docile minds by the official hierarchy. Bismarck said: "The preponderance of dynastic attachment, and the use of a dynasty as the indispensable cement to hold together a definite portion of the nation calling itself by the name of the dynasty is a specific peculiarity of the German Empire" ("Bismarck, the Man and the Statesman," vol. I, p. 322. Butter).

The late German Emperor is reported to have proclaimed: "There is only one master of the nation. And that is I, and I will not abide any other." . . . "I need Christian soldiers, soldiers who say their Pater Noster. The soldier should not have a will of his own, but you should all have but one will and that is my will; there is but one law for you and that is mine." The English nation quickly resented the claim to the divine right of kings and settled the question promptly and finally, very soon after the "right" was proclaimed to it.

assertion, exhibiting itself as initiative, enterprise, impatience of control. The Normans, a pure Nordic stock, exhibited this quality in a truly marvellous degree in their great age, when they conquered northern France, all England, Sicily, and much of Italy and of the Mediterranean coasts. For these astonishing feats were accomplished, not by the power of great highly organized states and immense armies of conscripts, slaves, or mercenaries, but by small bands of volunteers associated together for each particular enterprise under some chosen leader.

The anthropologists of the school of Le Play have offered a most interesting theory of the origin in prehistoric times of this very marked difference between the Nordic and the Alpine race. I have no time to put it before you.[1] But, whatever its origin, it must, I think, be accepted as one of the clearest and most important differences of racial quality. Are there, then, any recognized factors in human nature which may be the innate basis of this difference?

Yes. I have shown[2] that docility and self-assertion are rooted in two distinct and opposed

---

[1] I have given a condensed account of this theory in my "Group Mind."

[2] In my "Introduction to Social Psychology."

instinctive tendencies, which I have proposed to call the instincts of submission and of self-assertion respectively. I have shown reason to believe that the former is the root of all docility and suggestibility, that it is the principal factor in all those social phenomena which some authors have erroneously ascribed to the herd instinct.[1] And I have shown that the other, the instinct of self-assertion, is the most essential, the all-important factor, in what we call character, that complex organization from which spring all manifestations of will-power, all volition, resolution, hard choice, initiative, enterprise, determination.

If, then, we add to the qualities already assigned to the Nordic race an exceptional degree of strength of this instinct of self-assertion, and attribute to the Alpine race a stronger instinct of submission, we complete our hypothetical description of their racial qualities in a way which solves our present problem. It is this greater dose of self-assertiveness in the Briton which leads other peoples to complain that he goes about the world as though it belonged to him; it is this which, in spite of his lack of method and organiza-

---

[1] *E. g.*, W. Trotter, in "Instincts of the Herd in Peace and War."

tion, has enabled him to "muddle through" the Napoleonic Wars, the Crimean War, the Indian Mutiny, the South African War, and, lastly, the Great War. It is this which, in spite of his lack of subtlety and sympathy and intellectuality, has enabled him to subdue and govern the 300,000,000 of India. And it is this, in combination with his other qualities, that has rendered him the successful colonist *par excellence*.

Let us note in passing that the addition of this quality to the picture of the Nordic race completes, or makes more adequate, our explanation of the distribution of the Protestant religion in the world; for it shows us that the men of this race are by nature Protestants, essentially protesters and resisters against every form of domination and organization, whether by despot, church, or state.

Now consider for a moment the question of differences of innate moral qualities between more widely unlike races. We have found evidence of such moral differences where there is no evidence of differences of intellectual level, and between races closely allied and of similar civilizations. Is it not probable that, between races which show marked differences of intellectual capacity and which, in physical qualities and in level and type of culture, are widely different, there may be still larger differences of innate moral qualities? I think it is highly probable. But I do not feel competent to say much on this head. One would need an intimate acquaintance with extra-European civilizations, such as I cannot claim.

I would point out that, in respect of the peoples which have evolved no distinctive culture of their own, any reply to this question is peculiarly difficult, just because they lack the developed traditions and institutions which, as I have argued, give the best and clearest expression to the native qualities of any developed nation. But consider a single striking instance of such difference of moral quality—the difference between the Red man and the Black. Consider the difference of their relations to the Whites, throughout the history of this country. The Negro has in a way adapted himself to the position imposed upon him. He has multiplied, in spite of the ravages of disease,[1] both in slavery and freedom. But the Red man has never let himself be impressed into the social system of the dominant Whites; in some peculiar way he has proved resistant; he dies

---

[1] It is well known that alcohol, tuberculosis, and syphilis have taken a heavy toll of both Red and Black.

rather than submit. Does not this imply some deep-seated moral difference between the two races? If the Red man had the adaptability of the Negro, would he not have become a very important factor in the history of these United States of America? The same difference has appeared clearly throughout the West Indies, where the more adaptable black race has superseded the red men, even more completely than in this country. I am not sufficiently acquainted with the two races to attempt to define the racial qualities which have determined this difference. I will suggest merely, on the basis of a slight knowledge: (1) that the Negro race is pronouncedly extrovert, and that the red men are equally extreme introverts; (2) that the black race is more strongly gregarious and sociable; (3) further, that the red race is strongly self-assertive, while in the Negro the submissive impulse is strong. The last point may be illustrated by a true story of a Negro maid, whose Northern mistress, after treating her with great forbearance for a time, in spite of shortcomings, turned upon her and scolded her vigorously. The maid showed no resentment, but rather showed signs of a new satisfaction, and exclaimed: "Lor', Missus, you do make me feel so good." Is not this a typical and significant incident? I will even venture to suggest that, in the great strength of this instinct of submission, we have the main key to the history of the Negro race. In its own country it has always been ruled by absolute despots, who have obtained the most abject submission from their subjects, even when they have ruled with the utmost cruelty. These despots have often been men of foreign blood, Arabs largely. When Negroes have been well handled, with firmness but with kindness and consideration, as by the French officers who have trained the black regiments of France, they have proved themselves to be capable of extreme courage, devotion, and loyalty; to be, in short, ideal followers.[1]

---

[1] Cf. "Le Courage," by Voivenel and Huot, Paris, 1918. Shaler (op. cit.) insists upon the imitativeness and the eminent faithfulness of the Negroes to their white masters, and upon their sympathetic responsiveness; they "have the whole range of primitive sympathies exceedingly well-developed. They have a singularly quick, sympathetic contact with the neighbor; they attain to his state of mind and shape themselves to meet him as no other primitive people do. Those who have had a chance to compare in this regard the Negro and the American Indian must have been struck by the difference between the two peoples in this most important feature." Intimate contact with Oceanic Negroes (in the Torres Straits) and with Malays during many months impressed me strongly with the

The extreme facility with which the pure Negroes adopt the most extravagant superstitions, and the great influence of these upon their conduct—these facts point to and support the same assumption, namely an exceptional strength of the submissive instinct, the root of all docility and suggestibility.

There is a moral difference which distinguishes most of the peoples of primitive culture from those which have developed or acquired civilization; this, though it is difficult to explain, seems to be of the first importance. It may be defined as the difference between providence and improvidence. Improvidence is marked in the Malay

---

magnitude of this same difference between these outlying branches of these two races. Shaler points also to another striking difference between the black man and the red. He asserts that the Negro is much more capable of sustained labor, and he connects this with the fact that the Negroes have long practised a rude agriculture, while the ancestors of the red men were hunters and nomads. It seems to me doubtful whether this difference is rooted in innate or racial qualities. Any disposition to sustained labor is certainly conspicuous by its absence in the Oceanic Negroes with whom I am acquainted. It is difficult to conceive of such a disposition as an hereditary quality; this difference between Black and Red in America may well be due to the different conditions of life of the two races in the present and in the recent past.

and the Negro, the two tropical races *par excellence;* in less degree, perhaps, in the peoples of India (it is said that the Hindu family habitually squanders extravagant sums on such ceremonials as weddings and funerals); and in the Polynesian, Indonesian, and Melanesian; in fact, in all the races which have long inhabited the tropic regions, where man can survive without taking much thought for the morrow.

The opposite quality, providence, on the other hand, is shown in a high degree by all the peoples that have developed a high civilization. If we look more closely at these qualities, we see that improvidence is a negative quality; it is due to the absence of something which makes a man provident. Is this merely a matter of intelligence and imagination? I think not. The imagination of the Negro race seems to be vivid and powerful. It may be true that many of the improvident races are of rather low intellectual capacity. But a man may be extremely provident, in fact a real miser, in spite of a low degree of intelligence.

If a man is to be provident, he must be so constituted as to find some satisfaction in possession; that is to say, there must be in him an impulse to save or hoard which finds satisfaction in the act of hoarding, an impulse which prompts him to postpone enjoyment of the pleasure of immediate use to the satisfaction of possession. Such an impulse is shown by many animals, and I have claimed it as a true instinctive tendency of human nature.[1]

The strength or weakness of this tendency is, I suggest, the main factor in determining that a man or a race shall be provident or improvident. And it is very easy to see how natural selection may have developed this quality in peoples inhabiting cold or arid regions. It seems, in fact, to be present in the principal races in proportion to the demand for it made by their habitat. It seems to be strong in the Alpine and the Nordic race and in the Chinese; less strong in most branches of the Mediterranean; but strong in the Semites, in the Jews and Arabs and the Phœnicians, who long inhabited the dry desert regions.[2] Its strength seems to be a quality essential to any people that is to build up a civilization based on

---

[1] "Social Psychology."

[2] I may add that while writing these pages I have received from Australia a letter informing me of the opinion of the greatest living authority on the black natives of that continent; to the effect that the race is extremely deficient in, or wholly innocent of, the acquisitive impulse.

the accumulation of wealth, on commerce and industry, as every higher civilization has been. Owing to this necessity, every communistic or socialistic scheme which would abolish private property is an empty dream, an unrealizable ideal, a Utopia. The strength of this impulse seems to vary widely even in nearly related peoples, and also from one family to another. It would certainly seem to be stronger in the lowland Scotch than in the Irish; and it is, I think, not improbable that its variations are a principal ground of the social stratification which tends to arise in all acquisitive societies, that is to say, in all civilized peoples.

We have found reason to believe that, though the Nordic race has no monopoly of genius, though it does not excel, and perhaps does not equal, other races in many forms of excellence (as so extravagantly claimed by the race-dogmatists), it yet has certain qualities which have played a great part in determining the history, the institutions, the customs and traditions, and the geographical distribution of the peoples in whom its blood is strongly represented.

With two exceptions (namely differences of intellectual stature, and those subtle peculiarities of nervous constitution which determine extroversion and introversion) all the peculiarities we have assigned hitherto to races have been degrees of strength of certain instinctive tendencies.

We must ask—Are there other innate inherited qualities, besides these instincts which in their sum and balance are so large a part of the basis of moral development or character? The answer clearly is—Yes. We know that individuals differ in such things as musical and mathematical talent; and we know, also, that these talents are hereditary, and that, in respect of musical talent at least, there are marked differences between peoples. For example, no one can question the fact that the Welsh people is (statistically) more musically gifted than the English.

The innate basis of such talents is a very obscure matter; we do not know whether such a talent is an hereditary unit-quality or not. Probably it is complex. But we really are in almost total ignorance. I mention these special endowments, in order to enforce the contention that the innate basis of the mind may be far richer and more complex than is commonly assumed by the psychologists.

One medical psychologist of great experience and repute, Doctor C. G. Jung, has been led by many years devoted to deep exploration of the minds of nervous patients to believe that the innate basis of the mind comprises much that is specific and differentiated; he has revived the theory of innate ideas. He believes that each of us inherits what he calls "the collective unconscious," a part of the mind which manifests itself most clearly in dreams and in states of mental disorder, but which colors and biases all our thinking. This "collective unconscious" reveals itself chiefly in certain "archetypes," ideas which have a wide symbolical function, images which stand for or symbolize certain universally recurring relations and problems of human life. He holds that, though certain older and most fundamental of these "archetypes" are common to the whole human race, each race and each people that has lived for many generations under or by a particular type of civilization has specialized its "collective unconscious," differentiated and developed the "archetypes" into forms peculiar to itself.

He claims that in many cases he can discover the racial origins, the blood, of his patients by studying the forms of symbolism and the allegorical figures which appear in their dreams. He claims even that sometimes a single rich dream has enabled him to discover the fact, say, of Jewish or Mediterranean blood in a patient who shows none of the outward physical marks of such descent. And he finds these "archetypes" expressed in the mythology and folk-lore of each people, as well as in their dreams.[1]

Clearly, if these views of Doctor Jung are well founded, they are of the first importance for our topic; they would carry the doctrine of racial peculiarities of mental constitution much farther than I have done so far. I wish that I could give you a confident opinion for or against Jung's doctrine. The interest and importance of these views has seemed to me so great that I have put myself into the hands of Doctor Jung and asked him to explore the depths of my mind, my "collective unconscious"; that is to say, having no well-marked symptoms of insanity or neurosis, I have assiduously studied my own dreams under his direction and with his help. And the result is—I "evermore came out by that same door wherein I went." I do not know. I cannot find grounds for a decided opinion. I seem to find in myself traces or indications of Doctor Jung's "archetypes," but faint and doubtful traces. Perhaps it is that I am too mongrel-bred to have clear-cut archetypes; perhaps my "collective unconscious"—if I have one

[1] *Cf.* his "Psychology of the Unconscious."

—is mixed and confused and blurred. One of Jung's arguments weighs with me a good deal in favor of his view. He points out that the famous theory of Freud, which he himself at one time accepted, is a theory of the development and working of the mind which was evolved by a Jew who has studied chiefly Jewish patients; and it seems to appeal very strongly to Jews; many, perhaps the majority, of those physicians who accept it as a new gospel, a new revelation, are Jews. It looks as though this theory, which to me and to most men of my sort seems so strange, bizarre, and fantastic, may be approximately true of the Jewish race.

Again, one cannot ignore the fact that Jung has a number of ardent disciples who hold his theory true, because they find it helpful in the treatment of their patients. In face of this situation, suspended judgment with an open mind is the only scientific attitude.

But, though in my opinion the evidence adduced by Jung in support of his theory of archetypal ideas is not such as should secure acceptance of the theory by all impartial inquirers, it is worth while to point out that we have no positive knowledge which is incompatible with the theory. It is true that the theory is hardly to be reconciled

with the Neo-Darwinian principle which is so
widely accepted, somewhat dogmatically, by
many biologists at the present time, the principle
which denies the possibility of the transmission
from generation to generation of the effects of
use, the gains of facility and function made by
the efforts of each generation. But, as I shall
presently insist, this principle is by no means
finally established. On the other hand, there is
a certain amount of vague evidence, beyond that
adduced by Jung, which makes in favor of some
such view as his. First, it is becoming generally
recognized by biologists that the Darwinian principle of selection is not in itself adequate to account for the evolution of the world of living
things, and especially that it is inadequate to
account for the evolution of the mental powers
of the human species. Secondly, popular opinion,
based upon a vast amount of vague and unana-
lyzed experience, is decidedly opposed to scientific
opinion in this matter. And in these obscure
regions the popular tradition is often more nearly
right than the opinion prevailing in the scientific
world at any particular phase of the development
of science. Scientific opinion is too apt to deny
the possibility of alleged forms of happening, on
the ground that we cannot understand how such

things can happen. It cannot be too strongly
insisted that denial on such ground is always un-
justified, and that it is especially unjustifiable in
the obscure realm of the human mind, about which
our positive knowledge is still so scanty and rudimentary. Popular opinion in this matter would
seem to be influenced chiefly by similarities in
mental traits (both moral traits and peculiar intellectual capacities and tendencies, such as forms
of wit, aptitudes for language study, for mechani-
cal contrivance, for imaginative flights) which
may often be observed in members of a family.
Such similarities may be plausibly attributed to
personal contact and imitation in many cases.
But in other cases this explanation will not apply;
yet the similarities may be very striking. Thirdly,
the larger school of psychoanalysts, who follow
Freud rather than Jung, find evidence of certain
constantly recurring symbols in dreams and fan-
tasies which, if the evidence is sufficiently good,
necessitate the assumption of innate factors in the
mind very similar to Jung's archetypal ideas.[1]

---

[1] I refer more especially to such symbolic images as the
snake. In other ways, Professor Freud's own theory of
the neuroses implies clearly the principle of inheritance
of racial experience, and Professor Freud, in his later
writings, has fully recognized this implication. In his

Fourthly, the perennial interest of children in certain kinds of objects (both real and fanciful) of which they have had no experience, but which must have figured much in the imaginations of their remote ancestors, seems to point to the inheritance by the race of some traces of such ancestral experience. It is difficult to account in any other way for the spontaneous and vivid interest of almost all European children in stories of fairies, goblins, ghosts, witches, wolves, bears, caves, and enchanted forests. Fifthly, the development of moral sentiments in many children, their resentment of injustice, their appreciation of honesty and truth-telling, and other such moral reactions, seems so spontaneous and untaught that it is difficult to believe that these moral reactions or moral sentiments are not, in some manner and degree, preformed or hereditary in their constitution. There seem to be large differences between chil-

"General Introduction to Psycho-analysis" he writes: "I am of the opinion that these *primal phantasies* . . . are a phylogenetic possession. In them the individual reaches out beyond his own life, into the experiences of antiquity. . . . It seems very possible to me that everything which is obtained during an analysis in the guise of phantasy . . . were once realities in the primeval existence of mankind, and that the imaginative child is merely filling in the gaps of individual truth with prehistoric truth."

dren in respect of the ease with which such moral sentiments develop under the influence of example and training. And if the opinion widely held by alienists and criminologists, to the effect that some children are by nature insusceptible of moral training, though not lacking in intelligence, if this opinion is not utterly baseless, it is strong evidence of the inheritance by the normal child of some preformed moral sentiments, some tendency for such sentiments to take form in the mind spontaneously, however much their development may need to be furthered by experience and moral training. Again, there seem to be national and racial differences in this respect which do not seem to be wholly explicable in terms of differences of national tradition. There are, for example, among both civilized and uncivilized peoples, some which are notoriously untruthful; some which are remarkably chaste, though not deficient in the sex impulse; some as remarkably unchaste.

A sixth kind of evidence, pointing in the same vague way to a greater complexity of the innate constitution of the human mind than is commonly recognized by science, is afforded by the testimony of many persons whose work has made them familiar with alien races and with cross-bred races. Thus, it is asserted by many experienced Anglo-

Indian officials that education of Hindus by the methods and materials used in European education is positively deleterious to their mental development. And it is widely asserted of some of the populations which have been formed by the blending of widely dissimilar races, that both the intellectual and moral development of the majority of individuals among such populations is seriously defective in some obscure and ill-defined way. It is often alleged that such persons reveal a fundamental lack of harmony in their character, an abnormal liability to moral conflict and disorder.[1]

I will venture to state tentatively the view to which all these vague lines of evidence seem to me to point. The innate basis of the mind is richer, more complex, than present-day science is willing to admit. On both the moral and intellectual sides the innate potentialities are richer, more various, and more specific, than can be described in terms of degrees of intelligence and degrees of strength of the several instinctive impulses. Just as that peculiarity which enables a man to become

[1] *E. g.*, "It is a common opinion, held by the blacks as well as by the whites, that an infusion of white blood increases the intelligence of the negro, while at the same time lowering his moral qualities." (N. S. Shaler, "The Neighbor.")

a great mathematician (or a great musician) is certainly innate and hereditary, though we cannot define or conceive in what this hereditary basis consists; so also the development of the highest moral character only proceeds upon the basis of a hitherto undefined innate and hereditary peculiarity.

This undefined innate basis of moral character is perhaps of all innate qualities the most valuable possession of any human stock. It is the innate basis of a quality which we may best name dependability or trustworthiness. This quality is no simple unit; it cannot be ascribed to the operation of any one instinct; and, though it implies intelligence, it is not closely correlated with high intelligence. In respect of this complex and vaguely defined quality, races and peoples seem to differ widely. Without its presence in a high degree, no people can achieve or sustain a high level of civilization. Consider how the punctual and efficient working of any one of our great public services implies a high degree of trustworthiness on the part of a vast number of persons. When we see a great mail-train glide, punctual to the minute, into the railroad depot, after traversing hundreds or thousands of miles of varied territory, after burrowing through mountains, crossing great rivers, winding through deep gorges, thundering across vast plains, we do not often sufficiently realize on how many human beings this achievement has depended, or how great demands on their trustworthiness it has made. It is because such services make these great demands that a people is justly proud of the efficiency, the punctuality, the freedom from accident, and the dependability of such great public services. It is for the same reason that some peoples, even among the civilized nations, seem to be incapable of maintaining efficient services of this kind. It is for this reason that, among many peoples which have established such services, the posts of critical responsibility are generally filled by foreigners, men of a different race which seems to be more highly endowed with this complex quality of trustworthiness. It is not too much to claim for this quality that it is more important than any other, intelligence not excepted, for the maintenance of a high level of civilization. If, in any people that has attained such a high level, this quality should decline (statistically) we might anticipate a corresponding decline in the efficiency of all its public services. We might expect to see its police force become corrupt, its courts of justice less efficient, its criminals bolder and more numerous, its postal deliveries irregular, its railroad trains unpunctual and subject to many accidents, its bankruptcies and commercial panics more frequent, its strikes more reckless; and in war, the supreme test, it would, in spite of much bravery and high intelligence, be relatively ineffective. This is admittedly the expression of a somewhat speculative opinion which cannot claim to be founded on scientifically established facts.

Another speculative question may be touched on here, namely—Is there any correlation between high intelligence and the possession of the more desirable moral qualities; that is, do these tend to "go together"; are highly intelligent persons (statistically) on the whole better equipped with moral qualities than less intelligent persons? Professor Terman[1] provides some evidence that there is positive correlation between intelligence and the possession of the better moral qualities, and one of considerable degree. If this result is accepted it does not necessarily follow that the correlation is hereditary; but it is difficult to account for it in any other way. If such hereditary correlation were established, it would be a fact of the very first importance; for the methods of measuring

---

[1] "Intelligence of School Children," p. 58.

intelligence, which have been proved to be trustworthy by so many extensive researches of recent years, would then provide an indirect measure of the moral qualities, which, though fallible in individual cases, would be statistically trustworthy.[1]

I mentioned Doctor Jung's theory of archetypes, not only because it serves as a warning against dogmatic negation,[2] but because it raises in an acute form two closely allied questions that are of prime importance for our main topic—namely, the question of the persistence of peculiarities of mental endowment, and the question of the modes and influences by which they undergo change.

---

[1] I have found only one other piece of evidence directly supporting Professor Terman's. Mr. H. V. Race ("A Study of a Class of Children of Superior Intelligence," *Journal of Educational Psychology*, 1918), by the aid of mental tests, selected from a large number of children twenty-one who showed the highest degree of intelligence. He then studied these twenty-one children intensively and concluded that "they are apt to be unusually able in various fields of human learning," and "they are highly social in the scientific sense of the term. They tend to have good dispositions and lend themselves generously to the needs of the group."

[2] A warning especially important in view of the fact that some reactionary psychologists are showing a tendency to revert to the old view that the innate basis of the mind comprises nothing more than a number of simple reflex tendencies.

Before turning to these topics, let me sum up on the differences of innate mental qualities which seem to be well-founded rather than speculative assumptions. We have seen that the three great races of Europe seem to have possessed distinctive moral qualities, that these are, just like the physical qualities of those races, represented in the modern peoples in various degrees and combinations, according to the proportions in which they inherit the blood of these three chief races. We have no evidence that these races, or the peoples formed by their partial blendings, differ in degree of intellectual capacity. But, nevertheless, in their highest achievements, in the production of which intellect and character cooperate, we see evidences of qualitative differences in the working of their minds—in art and religion and politics, as we have seen, and I think we may safely add in philosophy and science. In these most purely intellectual spheres, general differences are widely recognized and may, I think, be attributed to the same moral peculiarities, subtly influencing and moulding the national traditions of thought. The clearness and perfection of expression of the French and Italians, their preference for logical order and the deductive principle, their formalism, their rationalism—

these are traditional national characteristics. They seem to be connected with the impetuousness, the immediacy of expression, and the strong sociability of the Mediterranean race; for these have moulded the languages into instruments of vivid clear-cut logical communication.

The strength of the English intellect is its empiricism, its constant appeal not to established and clearly formulated principles from which it may deduce conclusions, but rather to new facts. It constantly goes out, like the pioneers so well described by Volney, alone and unconcerned by its loneliness, its detachment from all intellectual precedent and companionship, and looks for new facts and new explanations, without feeling the need of fitting these into the framework of a single logical and consistent system.

The German intellect shows the reflective persistency of the introversion common to its two chief constituent races; in its strong regard for system and organization, in its tendency to accept as true whatever is socially and officially recognized as part of the system of thought, it reveals the submissive and highly sociable tendencies; while it lacks something of the clearness of the Mediterraneans and of the pioneering independence and empirical curiosity of the English.

We have found reason to believe that men and races differ in their innate mental constitution, on both the intellectual and the moral sides. Do such peculiarities persist through hundreds, perhaps thousands, of generations? Or is the innate basis of the mind plastic, easily transformed? Can a few generations of intellectual education and moral training appreciably modify or improve the innate constitution of any population?

The answer depends upon the answer to an unsolved biological problem, the most urgent of all the biological problems; one the answer to which profoundly concerns every state, and especially these United States of America; for many great questions of public policy should be determined largely by the answer to this biological problem, the problem—Are acquired qualities transmitted from one generation to another? The two great English founders of the modern theory of evolution, Darwin and Spencer, believed in such transmission. But at present the majority of biologists say—No. This negation is based upon, deduced from, a theory of a German professor, Weissman, a theory which may or may not be true. Now, one good result of the Great War is that we have broken away from the thraldom to theories of German professors to which the scientific world submitted before the war; and this particular theory is already less confidently held. The theory can be tested and the problem can be solved by intelligently directed experiment.[1]

Such research must occupy some years at least, and in the meantime we have a vast amount of printed matter but no decisive facts to go upon. But from many biological facts we can make this inference with some confidence. Innate qualities are in the main very persistent; and, even if modifications or qualities acquired by use are transmitted, the accumulation of such effects is in most, probably all, cases a very slight and slow and gradual process, requiring many generations to produce an appreciable degree of effect.

The persistence of physical qualities is most impressive. We have portraits of Egyptians who lived many thousand years ago, which closely resemble living men of the same region. We have instances of isolated patches of population which, amid all the shiftings and blendings of European

---

[1] I may say that in Harvard College we have put in hand a long experiment which should eventually give us a definite answer to this profoundly important problem —on one condition—namely, that we can secure the small funds needed to carry the experiment through to its conclusion.

peoples, seem to have remained unchanged in physical type for many thousands of years (*e. g.*, the island of population of the Cro-Magnon type in the Dordogne region of France[1]). We have the curious fact that the blood of various races shows chemical reactions peculiar to each race. As Professor Ripley says: "The persistence of ethnic peculiarities through many generations is beyond question" (page 120). On the other hand, there are instances in which change of habitat or of mode of life seems to have produced a slowly accumulating change of racial qualities; *e. g.*, life in hill country and life in complex civilized communities—both these seem in the course of many generations to produce somehow a raising of the cephalic index, that is, a relative broadening of the skull.

We must therefore compare branches of the same race which have lived widely apart; if these remain alike, and if also branches of unlike races which have long lived under similar conditions continue to show in full their racial differences, then we have good evidence of persistence of racial qualities in spite of environmental influences. Such instances are known. The Negro race has long lived in widely separated areas—in Africa,

---

[1] *Cf.* Ripley's "Races of Europe," p. 179.

Malaysia, the West Indies, North and South America. Yet it continues to show in all these areas the same fundamental physical qualities, and, what is more important, the same mental qualities. And in Malaysia and the Pacific we see populations of Malay and of Polynesian and of Negro blood which have long lived under well-nigh identical conditions, and which nevertheless continue to exhibit in full degree the physical and the mental differences of these races. These facts were pointed out by A. R. Wallace, and I have myself observed them. Some of you may assent easily to the view that physical qualities are very persistent; but may find it difficult to accept the same view of mental qualities. For bones and skulls are solid tangible objects; they seem durable and persistent. But how can such intangible immaterial entities as mental qualities persist unchanged for thousands of years? Well, even the qualities of the bony framework are handed down in an utterly mysterious manner, which biologists try to make a little less mysterious by invoking the "continuity of the germ-plasm." And the transmission of mental qualities is no more and no less mysterious than that of physical qualities. But it is well to realize that such mental qualities as the instincts are among the most durable things we know. The great instincts common to most of the higher animals were evolved long before mountain ranges such as the Alps assumed their present form; and they may well survive when all the mountains that we know shall have been worn away.

Indirect evidence and general considerations point to the great persistence of innate mental qualities, even under changed conditions. The early descriptions of the moral qualities of the inhabitants of Europe and especially of Gaul, which have come down to us from Tacitus and Cæsar and others, seem to show that the Nordics and the Alpines and the Mediterraneans of that time were distinguished by the same peculiarities which mark them now and which, throughout the historic period, have played their parts in determining the forms of their art, of their customs, and of their institutions.

Even the evidence of Jung and his disciples, which perhaps is the best evidence we have of the gradual modification of innate mental qualities by transmission of the effects of use, is nevertheless at the same time evidence of the strong persistence of such qualities. For the observers of this school claim to be able to trace in living men the influences of customs and ways of thinking which seem to have been impressed on the race thousands of years ago and which have persisted in spite of all the vicissitudes of the peoples of Europe in the historic period.

Is there any evidence of the opposite kind, pointing to rapid change and plasticity of the racial mental constitution? It is difficult to find any. One popular fallacy which is commonly accepted as such evidence we may dispose of in a few words. It is often supposed that the superiority of civilized man to his savage forefathers is an innate superiority, which he owes to his long-continued subjection to the influences of culture. It is agreed by those who have considered the matter that there is no good ground for this belief. The superiority of civilized man consists in, or arises in the main from, the fact that he has at his command all the accumulated resources and traditions of civilization. There is no good evidence for the belief that he is in any way innately superior to his savage ancestors. In fact, the probability seems to be that he is (statistically) inferior.

VI

WE are now in a position to return a considered answer to the question as to the influence of innate racial qualities upon the course of national life, which we formulated concretely in our second lecture. You will remember that we put the question in this form. If every infant of one nation were substituted for one of another nation, until the two peoples were completely exchanged, what effects would this substitution have upon their subsequent history? Let us imagine this to have been done in the year 1200 A. D. to the French and British peoples. Obviously, there would have been produced no sudden or violent change of the course of national life in either country. But would there not have taken place a gradual change of customs, laws, and institutions in both countries, so that in many respects they would have approximated to one another; and then perhaps have diverged, after a crossing of their paths? Is it not probable, for example, that France would not only have conquered great areas of the earth, but would have held and peopled them, and that with her more ancient and

mature civilization she would have dominated
the world? Is it not probable that the national
institutions of France would have gradually acquired a more particularist or individualist form;
and that in England administration would have
become more centralized, the family more unified,
the laws in general less adapted to give free play
to individual initiative? Is it not probable that
the laws of England would have been codified,
and those of France left a chaos of precedents, of
judicial decisions, of legislative compromises, all
unrelated and unharmonized by any clear logical
principles or rational system?

Let me state more generally the view to which
all our evidence seems to point. Each people that
has attained a high level of civilization has done
so on the basis of the intellectual and moral qualities of the races which have entered into its composition. The combination of qualities peculiar
to each race was formed and fixed during long
ages of the prehistoric period, compared with
which the historic period of some 2,500 years is
very brief.

These native qualities are the capital, as it were,
with which a people sets out on the path of civilization. They are subject to only slow changes; but
they do change, if factors making for change con-

tinue to operate in the same direction during many generations. But, like all highly developed qualities of animals and plants, the qualities most necessary for the development and support of civilization are more readily subject to decay or diminution than to further development.

Each people is endowed with qualities which incline it to civilization of a particular type, and which render it capable of supporting a civilization of a given degree of complexity. Each progressive people thus tends to reach the limit of complexity of civilization which is prescribed for it by its innate qualities; when that limit is reached, it ceases to progress and is very liable to actual retrogression or decay. For under civilization its qualities tend to deteriorate, rather than to improve.

Let us now examine this last statement.

The influences which may produce changes of racial qualities are of three kinds.

(1) Reversion. This is a doubtful factor. It is held by some biologists that any highly developed race will deteriorate, if its qualities are not maintained by continued selection. And it is held that isolation of any race is necessary for the maintenance of its special qualities; for crossbreeding with other races tends to produce rever-

sion to the lower ancestral type. There is some reason to fear that the miscegenation which is going on so widely between human stocks is having this effect; and not only on theoretical grounds. There are some faint empirical indications of it; for example, the northern peoples of Europe are steadily losing their fair complexion—the average complexion is darkening; and, as the fair complexion is undoubtedly a recent specialization, this looks like a case of reversion. Possibly, then, reversion of mental qualities is also going on. But it is possible that this darkening of the complexion of the mixed populations of northern Europe is an effect of a selection which favors the darker strains; for these seem to be more resistant to the unfavorable influences of town and factory life.

(2) Transmission of acquired qualities, of the effects of use, is a possibility. If it is an actual factor, what must have been its most general effect under civilization? Which kind of life is more suited to develop to the utmost and, by much exercise, impress more strongly on a population the more valuable qualities—intelligence, independence, initiative, providence, the parental and altruistic tendency, curiosity, and trustworthiness (for these seem to be the most valuable of the fundamental innate qualities)? Which mode

of life, I ask, is more suited to develop these by exercise—that of the hunter, herdsman, warrior, cultivator, living in a well-defined social unit, such as a village community; or the life of a wage-laborer, a mill-hand, a shop-assistant or small clerk, in one of our highly civilized nations? There can be no doubt, I think, that the advantage is with the former more natural mode of life. We must remember that universal schooling is a recent and but partially achieved ideal, and that schooling is but an imperfect substitute for the education that a boy gets from living vividly the natural life. This factor, then, probably makes for deterioration, if it is operative at all.

(3) Selection. It is of the very essence of civilization that, as it progresses, it abolishes more and more completely the operation of the various forms of natural selection which in primitive peoples undoubtedly tend to maintain and promote the racial qualities. And, in our modern western nations, medical science, charitable organization, and protective legislation have pretty well achieved the abolition of natural selection.

Sexual selection may have helped to evolve the higher racial qualities. Under modern conditions, with the prevalence of monogamy and of the excess of females over males, it can hardly be operative. And modern feminism is withdrawing more and more of the best of the women from marriage and motherhood.[1]

Instead of natural and sexual selection, we have operative a number of forms of selection, all of which seem to be injurious to the race.

Military selection involves the death of many of the best and boldest; and it withholds other well-endowed men from early marriage, leaving that privilege to the physically and mentally defective.

Selection by the towns. The towns tend to attract the most vigorous, the most capable and enterprising of the young people of the countryside; in each generation they stream into the towns, leaving an inferior residue in the villages and farms. In New England, as in Old England, the phenomenon is so well known that it is needless to insist on it. But it is not so generally

---

[1] I have no space to show the facts and inferences, and must refer the reader to an essay by Mr. S. H. Halford on "Dysgenic Tendencies," in the volume on "Population and Birth-Control," edited by C. and E. Paul, New York, 1917. His conclusion is: "In any case there seems no other prospect, if the full feminist ideal be realized, than the entire extinction of British and American intelligence within the next two or three generations" (p. 232).

appreciated that the towns not only withdraw the best from the countryside, but destroy these selected strains. For a variety of reasons, the town population does not maintain itself. The great towns are vortices which suck in the best of the population; and, from the racial point of view, they destroy it, for they destroy its natural fertility.

This destructive dysgenic influence of the towns is a part of a wider phenomenon, namely, the operation of the *social ladder* which enables men to pass easily up or down the social scale. In all civilized societies, except those founded upon a rigid caste system, the social ladder exists; and every step forward in democratic organization, everything that throws the world more completely open to talent, that finds the right man for the right place and the square peg for the square hole, educational facilities, scholarships, personnel agencies—all such things contribute to the perfection of the social ladder by which the ascent of merit and the descent of ineptitude are made easy.

Now an effective social ladder in any nation is a most important agency for the advancement of its civilization. In its absence, talent will not find due scope; the men who, by reason of superior

endowments, are its naturál leaders will not come
to the front. And that such men should be produced by a people and should achieve a due influence upon and leadership in every form of activity,
in government, in science, in art, in commerce
and industry, is the most essential condition of
national prosperity and national progress.[1] Hence
the nation with the best social ladder, other things
being the same, will for a time progress most
rapidly.

The social ladder tends to produce a social
stratification; it tends to a differentiation of
society into superimposed strata of unequal value.
That this has actually occurred is indicated by the
few experimental observations which I put before
you in support of the proposition that degrees of
intelligence are hereditary. We need many more
such investigations.[2] But the fact is shown by

---

[1] This position is argued at some length in my "Group
Mind."

[2] Mr. A. W. Kornhauser has recently provided fresh
evidence in a paper on "The Economic Standing of
Parents and the Intelligence of Their Children" (*Journal
of Educational Psychology*, vol. IX, 1918). He examined
1,000 children, drawn from five schools of the city of Pittsburgh. Of these schools A and B were attended chiefly by
the children of the poorer classes, largely unskilled manual
workers; C and D by children of a more prosperous class,

common observation also; the process has gone
farthest in the country in which the social ladder
has been longest in effective operation. Of European countries, England is that country; hence we
find that, as various observers have said, England
is a land of great contrasts; and the top stratum in
England, the upper professional and commercial

---

largely skilled artisans and small shopkeepers; E by children of parents in very comfortable circumstances. He
found that the groups from A and B "show a very large
proportion of Retarded, with an almost negligible number of Advanced"; C and D groups "have the most
nearly normal distribution of Retarded and Advanced";
the E group "shows the opposite tendency from the first
two schools (A and B), namely, a very small proportion
of Retarded, with a comparatively large percentage of
Advanced pupils. These data in themselves give some
indication of the marked association between economic
status and school advancement, and undoubtedly would
be much more striking if the different schools had a system of uniform grading; for there can be no question that
there is a tendency for the general lower ability in the
poor school to be compensated by a general lower standard of grading and *vice versa* in the wealthier school."
That is to say, if the several schools had the same standard
of grading, the superiority of intelligence of the children
of school E over the others (and of schools C and D over
A and B) would be revealed even more strikingly. The
same observer obtained a similar result by a different
procedure. Taking the possession of a telephone in the
home as an indicator of good economic status of the

classes, together with the aristocracy, which is constantly recruited from them (and from America), is probably richer in valuable human qualities than any other large human group now existing—or was so before the war; while the lower strata contain a deplorable proportion of human beings of poor quality.[1]

parents, and dividing all the children into the three groups—Retarded, Normal, and Advanced—he found that the following percentages of these three groups had telephones in the home: of the Retarded 19 per cent; of the Normal 32 per cent; of the Advanced 50 per cent. These facts afford valuable confirmation of the observations on the correlation of intelligence with social status, set out in the second lecture. For in this case the estimation of the intelligence of the children was made by the schoolteachers. The terms Retarded and Advanced mean that the child is below or above the school grade in which the average age is that of the child in question. This question is so important that it seems worth while to add the table showing the percentages of the three classes—Retarded, Normal, and Advanced—in the five schools respectively.

	Retarded	Normal	Advanced
A.................	45.2	47.1	7.7
B.................	36.7	55.9	7.4
C.................	29.4	50.4	20.2
D.................	28.8	51.7	19.6
E.................	12.7	62.7	24.6

[1] *See* Appendix II.

That is to say, the operation of the social ladder tends to concentrate the valuable qualities of the whole nation in the upper strata, and to leave the lowest strata depleted of the finer qualities.

This provides the leadership and ability required for the flourishing of national life in all its departments, and in so far is good and beneficial. But the working of the social ladder has further and less satisfactory results. The upper strata, which contain in concentration the best qualities of the nation, and which are capable of producing a far larger proportion of men fitted for leadership than the lower strata, become relatively infertile. The causes are varied and complex, and in the main psychological: late marriage, celibacy, and restriction of the family after marriage are the main factors.[1] This is not a new phenomenon or peculiar to any one or a few countries. It is a well-nigh universal phenomenon. Roughly, it may be said to be due to the outstripping of in-

---

[1] Herbert Spencer assumed that there was a natural physiologically grounded inverse correlation between fertility and intellectual development. It may safely be said that there is little or no ground for this assumption. The inverse correlation is well marked, but it is grounded in psychological rather than physiological factors, and is therefore subject to rational control and voluntary choice.

stinct by intelligence in these favored classes; for
instinct cares for the race; intelligence, save in its
most enlightened forms, for the individual.   It is
not confined to the topmost stratum.   It begins
there and descends through the strata immediately below.   In Britain it has reached the skilled-
artisan class, the pick of the wage-earning class,
and is displayed acutely in that class.   Mean-
while the lowest strata continue to breed at a
more normal rate; the birth-rate remains highest
among the actual mental defectives.[1]   The residua
in the villages continue to be drained more completely of their best elements; the towns sift out
the best-endowed of these immigrants and pass
them up the social scale to become sterilized by
their success.   The process tends to accelerate
and accentuate itself as it continues.   Thus, the
increasing demands of a civilization of progressing

---

[1] The present situation may be roughly described by
saying that the superior half of the population is ceasing
to produce children in sufficient numbers to replace their
parents, while the lower half continues to multiply itself
freely and is the source of all increase of population.   The
same statement is probably roughly true of America.   The
phenomenon is world-wide.   As Mr. Halford says (*loc.
cit.*): "The higher races are using the resources of scientific knowledge to reduce the death-rate of the inferior
peoples and the birth-rate of the superior."

complexity are for a time met by the operation of
the social ladder. But it is a process which cannot continue indefinitely. There must come a
time when the lower strata, drained of all their
best strains, can no longer supply recruits who
can effectively fill the gaps in the upper strata
and serve as efficient leaders in all the arts and
sciences of civilization. With increasing demands
and diminishing supply, a point must be reached
at which the supply falls short. That is the climax, the culminating point of the parabola of that
people; when a people reaches that point, it stands
at the height of its career, but it stands on the
brink of the downward plunge of the curve.

It seems to me highly probable that several of
the great nations are approaching or have reached
that point. I believe that Great Britain has gone
farther than any other; just because the development of democratic institutions has proceeded
more uninterruptedly and successfully and for a
longer time than in any other people; and also
because her stock has been depleted by emigra-
tion of vast numbers of persons of more than
average vigor and quality. But British complacency refuses to see the signs. In a recent leading
article *The Times* solemnly repudiated any such
notion, asserting that the nation which in the

past has thrown up so much ability, so many great men, will not fail to produce the men needed to meet all future demands.[1]   The fatuous belief in the old dictum, that the great occasion or the great need always brings forth the great man to lead the nation over its difficulties, should have been shaken by the Great War.   For one of the most striking facts of that prolonged struggle was the failure of the nations involved to bring forth great men adequate to their needs.   Did not every nation, France alone excepted, fail to produce a great commander by land or sea?   Did any nation produce a great statesman?   You may say that the problems were harder, the times more difficult, than ever before; that the inadequacy of men was relative only to the vastness of the needs.

---

[1] The *London Times*, May 19, 1920.   After citing from the report of the registrar-general, which showed clearly the relative infertility of the educated classes, the editorial runs: "We are amused rather than dismayed by the prophets of 'racial suicide' and have complete confidence in the capacity of the English stock to respond to all the needs of the future."   This fatuously complacent utterance was presumably written by a man educated at Oxford, the university whose leading objects of study are history and the writings of Plato, the most thorough-going eugenist of all the social philosophers.   And it was written after the Great War, which has done incalculable and irreparable injury to the British stock.

Perhaps it was so, though I think not. But granting this, does not the fact remain an illustration of the law that the demands of civilization tend to outrun the qualities of its bearers?

During the years of the French revolution and the Napoleonic wars, many soldiers rose from the ranks to become great generals. During the industrial revolution in England many men rose from the ranks to eminence and high command, men like George Stephenson, and many others of his stamp.

But the social ladder has been at work for several generations since these men rose, and with fatal efficiency. Such rising has become much rarer in the old countries, in spite of the increased encouragement offered in the way of education and rewards.[1] And is it clear that you in America are in a better position? It is true that your population is recruited largely by immigration. But these million-a-year immigrants are untested material; they are an uncertain quantity.[2] In the old days men and women did not

[1] This fact is brought out by Mr. Havelock Ellis's "Study of British Genius."

[2] I remind you that two observers have found the children of Italian immigrants to be decidedly lower in the scale of intellectual capacity than those of the older white population.

emigrate to America, unless they were persons of more than average vigor, initiative, enterprise, and independence. But the steamship companies, and the spread in this country of civilization and of immigrants from all parts of the world, have altered all that. And your social ladder works with great efficiency; while the rule of the infertility of the selected classes seems to be rigidly maintained.[1]

You in New England cannot maintain the

---

[1] And the old stock is dying out. Mr. L. Quessel reviews the evidence of "Race Suicide in the United States" in an essay in the volume on "Population and Birth-Control" (edited by C. and E. Paul) and concludes: "All available data combine to prove that the Anglo-American population has not merely attained its maximum, but has already begun to decline." He adds: "It is perfectly clear that the low birth-rate among the Anglo-American population is not the result of natural sterility, but is due to a deliberate restriction of births."

In this all-important matter of birth-control the position of this country is remarkable and uniquely disastrous. The educated classes seem to cultivate and practise the principles of birth-control more assiduously than any other class of persons of the civilized world, while, *mirabile dictu*, they maintain laws which forbid the extension of the knowledge of such principles to the mass of the people. Doctor M. S. Iseman has drawn a lurid picture of this state of affairs in his "Race Suicide" (New York, 1912).

fatuous complacency of the editor of the *London Times!* For you have first-hand knowledge of old and formerly valuable populations, now drained of all that was best and reduced to stagnation. You exemplify in the highest degree the rule of the infertility of the selected classes. You have

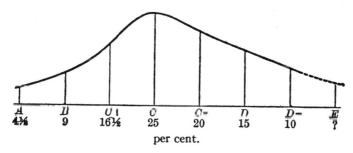

| A | B | U | C | C- | D | D- | E |
| 4¾ | 9 | 16½ | 25 | 20 | 15 | 10 | ? |

per cent.

The curve of distribution of intelligence in the young manhood of the American people, as revealed by army tests, runs as in the figure.

first-hand acquaintance with the process of substitution of population of one type by another, and with the consequent social effects. For you these things are not vague and fanciful possibilities; they are actual. They should lead you to concentrate your attention on these demographic problems.

Let me remind you of our curve of distribution of intelligence. Intelligence, as I said, is only one of many factors; but it is one of considerable importance.

A men are of the grade which "has the ability to make a superior record in college"; B men are "capable of making an average record in college." C men are "rarely capable of finishing a high-school course." And the main bulk of your population is below the C + level.[1]

---

[1] That is to say, the results of the army tests indicate that about 75 per cent of the population has not sufficient innate capacity for intellectual development to enable it to complete the usual high-school course. The very extensive testing of school-children carried on by Professor Terman and his colleagues leads to closely concordant results. He divides the children on the basis of his tests into the following classes (and it should be added that the school-status of the children and the judgments of their teachers bear out the grading very fully): Border-line cases (scoring 70–80 marks in the testing). These roughly correspond to the groups D − and E of the army tests, and are about 8 per cent of the whole number of school-children. Of these Professor Terman says: "According to the classical definition of feeble-mindedness, such individuals cannot be considered defectives. Hardly any one would think of them as institutional cases. Among laboring men and servant girls there are thousands like them. They are the world's hewers of wood and drawers of water. And yet, as far as intelligence is concerned, the tests have told the truth. These boys are uneducable beyond the merest rudiments of training. No amount of school instruction will ever make them intelligent voters or capable citizens in the true sense of the word. . . . It is interesting to note that [children of this grade] represent

The civilization of America depends on your continuing to produce A and B men in fair numbers. And at present the A men are 4 per cent, the B men 9 per cent; and you are breeding from the lower part of the curve. The A men and B men, the college-bred, do not main-

---

the level of intelligence which is very, very common among Spanish-Indian and Mexican families of the Southwest and also among Negroes. Their dulness seems to be racial, or at least inherent in the family stocks from which they come. The fact that one meets this type with such extraordinary frequency among Indians, Mexicans, and Negroes suggests quite forcibly that the whole question of racial differences in mental traits will have to be taken up anew, and by experimental methods." Above these comes the group of "dull normals" (scoring 80–90 marks). They constitute about 15 per cent of the whole number and correspond roughly to the D group of the army tests—"they are far enough below the actual average of intelligence among races of western European descent that they cannot make ordinary school progress." The third group is of "average intelligence" (scoring 90–110 marks) and comprises about 60 per cent of the whole number. "The high school does not fit their grade of intelligence as well as the elementary and grammar schools." They correspond roughly to the groups C −, C, and the lower part of C + of the army tests. Next comes the group of "superior intelligence" (scoring 110–120 marks). It comprises about 15 per cent of the whole, and corresponds to the upper part of group C + and to groups B and A of the army tests.

tain their numbers, while the population swells enormously.[1] If this goes on for a few generations, will not the A men, and even the B men, become rare as white elephants, dropping to a mere fraction of one per cent? It is only too probable.

The present tendency seems to be for the whole curve to shift to the right with each suc-

---

[1] Harvard graduates, it is said, have less than two children apiece on the average, and the same is probably true approximately of the graduates in general. With the graduates of women's colleges the case seems to be still worse. Professor J. McK. Cattell asserts: "Among the educated and well-to-do classes the number of children does not nearly suffice to continue the race. The Harvard graduate has on the average seven-tenths of a son, the Vassar graduate one-half of a daughter" (*Popular Science Monthly*, January, 1909). For a full revelation of the facts in regard to college women, see Popenoe and Johnson's "Applied Eugenics," chap. XII. Professor Karl Pearson has shown that the most prolific quarter of the population in Great Britain produces 50 per cent of the children of each generation. It is in the highest degree probable that this one-quarter belongs almost wholly to the right or inferior end of the curve.

In an article in the volume "Heredity and Eugenics" (Chicago, 1913) Doctor C. B. Davenport, one of the highest authorities on these matters, gives us the following interesting calculation. Writing of the graduates of Harvard College, he states: "At the present rate [of reproduction] 1,000 graduates of to-day will have only 50 descendants 200 years hence. On the other hand, recent cessive generation.[1] And this is probably true of moral qualities, as well as of intellectual stature. If the time should come when your A and B men together are no more than one per cent, or a mere fraction of one per cent, of the population—what will become of your civilization?

Let me state the case more concretely, in rela-

immigrants and the less effective descendants of the earlier immigrants still continue to have large families, so that from 1,000 Roumanians to-day in Boston, at the present rate of breeding, will come 100,000" after the same space of time, namely, 200 years. Blind optimists, confronted with the facts of the dying out of the old American stocks, are apt to remark that the rate of reproduction of the new immigrants will also decline. This is probably true of those among them who have the moral and intellectual capacity to climb the social ladder; but that is not a consoling reflection. Substitute for the 1,000 Roumanians of the foregoing calculation 1,000 mental defectives (and these are only a small fraction of the total number in the Boston area) and you have a more exact picture of the present tendency of change in the population. For the mental defectives are, it appears, the most persistently prolific class of the population, so long as they are left at liberty to do as they please.

[1] Since it has been shown that actual mental defectives are the most prolific part of the population, it is of some interest to estimate their numbers. Authorities give various estimates; for the class is not yet defined in any generally accepted manner. Most authorities seem to estimate them as above 2 per cent of the population in

tion to one of the great essential professions of which I have some inside knowledge, namely the medical profession. Two hundred or one hundred years ago, the knowledge to be acquired by the medical student, before entering upon the practice of his profession, was a comparatively small body of empirical rules. The advance of civilization has enormously multiplied this knowledge; and the very existence of our civilized communities depends upon the continued and effective application of this vast body of medical art and science. The acquiring and the judicious application of this mass of knowledge make very much greater demands upon the would-be practitioner than did the mastery of the body of rules of our forefathers. Accordingly, the length of the curriculum prescribed for our medical stu-

---

this country. Goddard, the highest authority in the matter, says: "It is a conservative estimate to declare that 2 per cent of public-school children are distinctly feeble-minded; . . . the most extensive study . . . of an entire school system of 2,000 has shown that 2 per cent of such children are so mentally defective as to preclude any possibility of their ever being made normal and able to take care of themselves as adults." Others have estimated the feeble-minded in the schools as high as 4 per cent. To these have to be added the declared defectives who are not sent to the public schools.

dents has constantly been drawn out, till now its duration is some six years of post-graduate study.

The students who enter upon this long and severe course of study are already a selected body; they have passed through high school and college successfully. We may fairly assume that the great majority of them belong to the A or B or at least the C + group in the army scale of intelligence.[1]

What proportion of them, do you suppose, prove capable of assimilating the vast body of medical knowledge to the point that renders them capable of applying it intelligently and effectively? If I may venture to generalize from my own experience, I would say that a very considerable proportion, even of those who pass their examinations, fails to achieve such effective assimilation. The bulk of modern medical knowledge is too vast for their capacity of assimilation, its complexity too great for their power of understanding. Yet medical science continues to grow in bulk and complexity, and the dependence of the community upon it becomes ever more intimate; for the natural resistance of the population to disease de-

---

[1] Or to Professor Terman's groups of superior and very superior intelligence.

clines, in proportion as the population is effectively protected by medical science from the selective action of diseases.

In this one profession, then, which makes such great and increasing demands on both the intellectual and the moral qualities of its members, the demand for A and B men steadily increases; and the supply in all probability is steadily diminishing with each generation.

And what is taking place in this one profession is, it would seem, taking place in all the great professions and higher callings. *Our civilization, by reason of its increasing complexity, is making constantly increasing demands upon the qualities of its bearers; the qualities of those bearers are diminishing or deteriorating, rather than improving.*

If we turn now to consider very briefly the history of the great peoples of the past, we find evidence which bears out my main thesis, which goes far to substantiate the explanation of the Parabola of Peoples suggested in these lectures.

The most glorious civilization of the past was that of ancient Greece. We do not know the ethnic composition of the people which produced that civilization. It is still a matter of dispute.[1]

---

[1] It has been maintained by many that it was predominantly Nordic. The most probable view seems to be

But we do know that the present population of
Greece is in the main of different stock.[1] And
history shows that the change or substitution of
population took place about the time of the
decay of that civilization. The causes of this
disaster were many. There was the psychological infertility of the selected classes, with the
decay of marriage and family life. There was
exile and colonization, both on a great scale; and
there was almost perpetual warfare, largely of
Greek against Greek; all tending strongly to the
elimination of the most fit. There was finally,
and on a great scale, exportation of Greeks by
their Roman conquerors, as slaves to do the clerical
and professional work of the Roman Empire. No
wonder that the collapse of that civilization, borne
by so small a population, was sudden and complete.

The grandeur that was Rome endured for a

---

that, like the English, the population of ancient Greece
was, in the main, a mixture and partial blend of the
Nordic and Mediterranean races, enriched by the attraction of many choice individuals from surrounding countries.

[1] Ripley ("Races of Europe," p. 407) shows that,
whereas the ancient Greeks were (statistically) long-
headed, the modern population is predominantly short-
headed, presumably owing to the predominance of Slavic
blood.

longer space. For it was founded upon a broader basis of population. During some centuries the Roman Empire drew into its service the best energies and talents of all the populations of Europe. Common soldiers from remote provinces rose to be emperors or governors; slaves imported from afar became secretaries of state and skilled administrators. The whole Empire was one great vortex, sweeping to its centre the best talents of the civilized world. All roads led toward Rome. And the rule of the infertility of the selected classes prevailed. Marriage became unfashionable, children were regarded as a burden. Pleasure, luxury, and the production of elegant Latin verse became the leading preoccupations of the selected classes. The Church, with her advocacy of celibacy and her doctrine that it is better to marry than to burn, lent her powerful aid. For many generations the process went on, the process of the extermination of the most valuable strains; in Otto Seeck's expressive phrase, the process of the "Ausrottung der Besten."[1] The mistress of the world reached the climax of her parabola and rapidly declined; and the chaos of the early middle ages succeeded.

---

[1] "Geschichte des Untergangs der Antiken Welt." See also Professor J. L. Myres, "Changes of Population in the Classical World," *Eugenic Review*, 1917.

The next great empire comparable to Rome's was that of Spain—a wonderful and brilliant career, but of short duration. The expulsion of the Moors and of the Jews, the work of the Inquisition, the celibacy of the Church, perpetual warfare, the drain of a vast colonial empire, and the luxury and wealth derived from it—all these combined to sap away the strains of finest quality; and the power and glory of Spain rapidly declined. France and England took up the struggle and fought for the mastery of the world.

Germany, coming relatively late under the devastating influences of our industrial civilization, has made her bid for world domination and has failed; and, incidentally, has left the battle-fields of Europe and the Near East strewn with the corpses of the best and bravest of our young men: brilliant young poets and scientists, inventors and authors and administrators, by the score and by the hundred are lying there, without descendants to perpetuate their talents, leaving the world forever poorer and the peoples of Europe diminished in moral and intellectual stature for all time.

Westward the march of empire takes its way, throwing out before it a vanguard of pioneers, of its best and brightest and most vigorous. Already the centre of gravity, of power, has passed by these Eastern States of America. The Middle West is already claiming predominance; and the day of the Far West is at hand. And after that—what?

The process has acquired a frightful rapidity and momentum. Every feature of your American civilization seems to conspire for its acceleration, for the more rapid attainment of the climax of your curve and the subsequent decline—every feature save one only.

What is this factor which alone can secure your future, and save you as a people from the fatal decline; which may even secure you a continued progress in all that makes the worth of human living?

It is the increasing knowledge of human nature and of human society, and of the conditions that make for or against the flourishing of human nature and society. But the mere increase of such knowledge in scientific academies is of no avail, if that knowledge is not widely diffused among the people, and if it does not become a guide to action in public and in private life.

Fortunately, in this country there is widely diffused a belief in the value of science and of its application to human life. You have many keen

workers adding to the sum of knowledge, and you
have a wide-spread tendency to be guided by it.
Therein lies your hope for the future. Such
knowledge is virtually a new factor in history.
And the essential problem before you is—Can
you as a nation so make use of this new factor,
this increasing knowledge of human nature and
human society, as to turn the course of history?
Can you by taking thought and action guided by
thought, can you prevent or indefinitely postpone
that decline of your curve of civilization which
seems even now to threaten you? I firmly believe that you, of all the existing nations, with the
possible exception of Japan, have the best prospect of achieving this mastery of your fate. What
steps you will take; what changes of law, of social
organization, of domestic institutions, you will,
upon mature consideration, institute, I do not
know and I do not suggest. To make any such
suggestions is no part of my task in this short
study. It is enough, if I have directed your attention to this supremely important problem; if I
have led you to see that every wide measure of
social legislation, every social custom and institution, should be judged and evaluated with reference to its bearing upon this problem—its probable effect on the anthropologic constitution of

the nation and the sum of its human qualities. All such laws and customs and institutions have their inevitable effects of this all-important kind. The laws regulating the sale of alcohol; the immigration laws; the laws of marriage and divorce; the educational system; the relations of labor to capital; the nature and degree of state-interference with personal liberty; the distribution of the population in town and village; the size and type of your cities—all these are but a few instances of influences capable of exerting subtle but profound effects upon the quality of the population of these United States of America.

But most important of all is the diffusion of the sense of individual responsibility in this matter; the clear realization that, in the last resort, the future will be the creation of the present, that the nation of the future must issue from the individual choice and action of those who now compose it.

APPENDICES

APPENDIX I

COMMENTARY ON THE PROPOSITION THAT ALL MEN ARE BORN WITH
EQUAL CAPACITIES FOR MORAL AND INTELLECTUAL
DEVELOPMENT

PORTRAITS OF THREE MEN ALL OF WHOM IN THEIR
YOUTH WERE DENIED THE ADVANTAGES
OF SCHOOLING AND THE REFINEMENTS
OF CIVILIZATION

This man, by virtue of his qualities of character and intellect, rose from a very humble station to a position of the highest responsibility and power. He so filled that position as to gain the unbounded admiration of all men and of all nations.

This man, my friend Tama Bulan, was the chief of a small village in the heart of Borneo. He and his people belonged to one of the tribes which have often been described as degraded savages, stigmatized as head-hunters, and erroneously stated to be cannibals. By reason of his high intelligence, his humane feeling, his firmness of character, and statesmanlike foresight, he acquired a great moral influence not only over the people of his own village and tribe, but over many of the other tribes throughout a large area. He used this influence to bring to an end the chronic tribal warfare which in all that region of the earth had long prevailed. By his influence and example he brought peace, happiness, and prosperity to many thousands of his fellow men. Some account of him and his people may be found in "The Pagan Tribes of Borneo," by Charles Hose and Wm. McDougall (London, 1912).

This man remained unknown to fame, until he was photographed by the authors of a recently published book[1] as a representative specimen of the inferior type of the Ila-speaking people. We are told nothing of his moral and intellectual qualities; but the most resolutely optimistic humanitarians will hardly claim him as a "mute inglorious Milton," or even as a "village Hampden." Nor is it easy to suppose that they could contemplate with equanimity the substitution of the Anglo-American stock by persons of this type.

[1] "The Ila-speaking People of Northern Rhodesia," by Rev. E. W. Smith and Captain A. M. Dale, London, 1920. I am indebted to Mr. Smith for the copy of the picture.

APPENDIX II

Birth-rate in the Social Strata

In Great Britain little has been done in the way of anthropometric survey by the methods of mental measurement. But there has recently been published a survey, by the method of personal interview and estimation, of a large sample of the "manual workers" of Sheffield ("The Equipment of the Workers," London, 1919). Sheffield is a typical manufacturing town of some half-million inhabitants, seated in Yorkshire, near the border of Lancashire; these two counties are noted for the vigor and achievement of many of their sons and daughters. The investigation dealt with 866 men and women in equal numbers. They were divided into three classes: A, the well-equipped; B, the inadequately equipped; C, the mal-equipped. Class A consists of men and women who, as judged by personal impression, by their mode of life and history, seem to be of character (often of fine character) and abilities such as enable them to cope with the problems of life in a satisfactory manner. Their personalities and life-histories may be contemplated with satisfaction, entire sympathy, and considerable admiration. If these were a fair sample of the "manual workers" of the whole country, Britain would be, indeed, a great and happy land. But, unfortunately, they constitute less than one-fourth of the whole group (about 22 per cent).

Class C constitutes one-fourteenth of the whole. They are a bad lot. "In stupidity or in ignorance or in base cleverness, those in this class live for ends of their own, in vicious ways that pollute the lives of others. From their loins come the intellectually feeble and the morally depraved children that sap all the best energies of the school-mistress."

Class B comprises all who fall between the levels of classes A and C. "These, in their scores of thousands in Sheffield, and in their millions upon millions in the whole country, are the real 'masses,' the real 'poor,' the real 'people.' . . . They manage to live their own lives and to keep quite as free as the average member of the well-to-do classes from vice and crime. What distinguishes them, or 'indistinguishes' them, so to speak, is their lack of positive qualities of any kind. . . . It is our honest belief that neither the man, nor—still more certainly—the woman, in Class II (*i. e.*, B) can in any genuine sense of the word be called 'fit to vote.'" They form 70 per cent of the "manual workers." Detailed notes on a score of individuals from each of the classes A and B are given, these being regarded as fair samples of the two classes. A careful comparison of the detailed descriptions of these samples from the two classes points, I think, clearly to the conclusion that the difference between Classes A and B is in the main one of intrinsic or innate quality, and cannot be ascribed to differences of training or educational opportunity. None of Class A (with one doubtful exception) had attended school beyond the fourteenth year; several of them are described as illiterate, or ignorant, or "never reads," or "scarcely any education." The average of schooling and home training is not appreciably less in Class B. Yet one is made to feel that the average "civic worth" of Class A is vastly greater than that of Class B. The authors of the volume imply (probably correctly) that the majority of the members of Class B might have been made into fairly satisfactory citizens, even made "fit to vote," if the social and educational conditions under which they grew up had been very much better than they actually were, if each one had been carefully trained and fully educated in a good school and home, and shielded from all degrading influences. But the striking fact remains that, of the "manual workers" of this representative group, nearly one-quarter grew to be good citizens, in spite of many adverse circumstances, while three-quarters of them failed so to grow. Would it not make a vast difference to the future of Britain, to the welfare and happiness of the whole population, and to the political stability, wisdom, and beneficent world-influence of the country, if the next generation of "manual workers" could come wholly from the loins of Class A. As the writers point out, the elimination of the relatively small Class C would bring the country in sight of Utopia. But other investigators have made it appear only too probable that Class C is the most prolific, and Class A the least prolific, of the three classes. Thus it has been shown that the birth-rate, among members of the Hearts of Oak Benefit Society, fell below 15 per 1,000, while that of the population at large remained a little above 30 per 1,000 (Chapple's "Fertility of the Unfit"). Now the members of the Hearts of Oak Society are in the main the pick of the "manual workers," just such persons as make up the Class A of the Sheffield "manual workers."

A strong inverse correlation of the birth-rate with social status seems to be general throughout the European nations. The proof of it in Great Britain and in the United States of America is overwhelmingly strong. Karl Pearson and his associates have proved it for London beyond question; especially David Heron ("On the Relation of Fertility in Men to Social Status," London, 1906) and Newsholme and Stevenson ("The Decline of Human Fertility," London, 1906). The last-named authors sum up by saying: "The figures show in a manner which hardly admits of any doubt that in London at any rate the inhabitants of the poorest quarters—over a million in number—are reproducing themselves at a much greater rate than the more well-to-do." A similar state of affairs was shown to obtain before the war in Holland, in Berlin, and in Vienna. In America the evidence is not so complete. But similar facts have been demonstrated for Pittsburgh. In that city "Ward 7 has the lowest birth-rate and the lowest rate of net increase of any ward in the city. With this may be contrasted the Sixth Ward. . . . Nearly 3,000 of its 14,817 males of voting age are illiterate. Its death-rate is the highest in the city. Almost nine-tenths of its residents are either foreigners or the children of foreigners. Its *birth-rate is three times*

that of the Seventh Ward. Taking into account all the
wards of the city, it is found that the birth-rate *rises*
as one considers the wards which are marked by a
large foreign population, illiteracy, poverty, and a
high death-rate. . . . The correlation between illiteracy and net increase is + .731. The net increase
of Pittsburgh's population, therefore, is greatest
where the percentage of foreign-born and of illiterates
is greatest. . . . Pittsburgh, like probably all large
cities in civilized countries, breeds from the bottom.
The lower a class is in the scale of intelligence, the
greater is its reproductive contribution." (P. Popenoe
and R. H. Johnson, "Applied Eugenics," New York,
1918, p. 138.)

The fact of the greater rate of increase of the poorer
classes (or, more generally, the inverse correlation of
fertility with good social status) is abundantly established; it cannot be denied by our resolute optimists
and fatuously complacent editors. When these people condescend to consider this fact, they usually take
the line that "one man is as good as another, and
sometimes a good deal better, too." They deny that
there is any correlation between position in the social
scale and intrinsic or native worth. It may be hoped
that the facts of correlation of intelligence with social
status, recited in the pages of this book, may lead such
persons to consider the problem more seriously. But
we need more evidence on the point.[1] It is much to

---

[1] The last resort of those who are unwilling to accept
the evidence of positive correlation between intelligence

be regretted that the Sheffield investigators seem to have paid no attention to the question of the birth-rate among their three classes. Children are men-

---

and good social status is to assert that the children of the better social classes are stimulated to more rapid intellectual development in their earliest years by contact with their more intellectual parents. This explanation has been fully considered and rejected by the workers who have obtained the evidence. I will merely point out here how little ground there is for this assumption. The children of the better social classes, especially perhaps in England, too often spend most of the waking hours of their early years shut away in a nursery, with little or no companionship beyond that of a dull nurse-maid, or sitting solemnly in a baby-cart which is pushed round and round some public park. The children of the poor enjoy in the main far more companionship, both childish and adult, have more stimulating contacts, are thrown more upon their own resources, and are much less inhibited and repressed. In consequence, they are notoriously precocious and sharp-witted in their early years; the London gamin is celebrated in this respect. The life of the street and the gutter may have many dangers, moral and physical, but it is at least stimulating. As Mrs. Dewey, a high educational authority, says in a recent article: "Not the least advantage of being born poor is the opportunity it offers for getting real experience in childhood" (*The Nation*, No. 2913). Perhaps no one but a parent who has lived intimately with his children, striving day by day and night by night to promote their development, can fully realize how refractory is the natural process of unfolding to all our efforts.

tioned, but the number is not stated in most cases—
an illustration of the blindness to this all-important
topic of so many earnest social workers.

Some years ago I made a rough census of the
families of such of the resident teachers of Oxford as
were known to me and my collaborators. This
group included 142 members of this highly intellectual selected class and may fairly be regarded as a
true sample. I found that each of these 142 men
had on the average 1.8 children; that is to say, 284
adults (142 married couples) had 261 children. A
few of these couples, being still comparatively young,
would produce more children; but of the then existing children some would die before becoming adults.
These two unknown quantities are probably not very
unequal. In estimating the reproduction rate of
this highly selected class, we must take into the
account the fact of the very large number of bachelors
within it, who, being well advanced in years, are not
likely to marry. It was easy to count 70 elderly
bachelors, all men of intellectual distinction.

APPENDIX III

The New Plan

What is to be done about it? That is the urgent question in the mind of every serious man or woman who understands the facts and is not utterly blind to the teachings of history. Many social philosophers from Plato onward have advocated measures for the preservation or improvement of racial qualities. Some of these, including Plato's stud-stable method and the practices of infanticide and abortion, which were common among the Spartans and other Greeks, cannot be approved or legally recognized to-day without grave danger of deterioration of our common morality, without loss of much of that improvement of the moral tradition which European civilization has undoubtedly achieved in the last two thousand years, and which we owe so largely to the teachings of the Founder of Christianity. Yet much can be done. Our aim in general must be to favor increase of the birth-rate among the intrinsically better part of the population, and its decrease among the inferior part. The first essentials are the further acquisition of knowledge of the facts and principles involved, a wide diffusion of such knowledge, and the building up of a strong public opinion. The second and third are now more important than the first; for, though more exact knowledge is desirable, we have sufficient to serve for sure general guidance.[1]

The firm and sufficient basis of the demand for eugenic measures is the long-recognized fact that you may not expect to gather figs from thistles or grapes from thorns. More explicitly it may be stated as follows: Human qualities, both mental and physical, are hereditary; and any human stock is capable of being improved by training and education, by good environmental influences, very slowly only, if at all, and probably not at all. Human beings, far from being born with equal potentialities of moral and intellectual development, inherit these in very different degrees. Any population may in principle be regarded as consisting of two halves; the half made up of all individuals the sum of whose innate qualities or potentialities is above the average or mean value, and the

---

[1] Messrs. Popenoe and Johnson say: "The basal differences in the mental traits of man (and the physical as well, of course) are known to be due to heredity, and little modified by training. It is therefore possible to raise the level of the human race—the task of eugenics—by getting that half of the race which is, on the whole, superior in the traits that make for human progress and happiness, to contribute a larger proportion to the next generation than does the half which is on the whole inferior in that respect. Eugenics need know nothing more, and the smoke of controversy over the exact way in which some trait or other is inherited must not be allowed for an instant to obscure the known fact that the level can be raised." (*Op. cit.*, p. 114.)

fort

other half made up of individuals the sum of whose qualities is below the mean value. If these two halves have persistently unequal birth-rates (and the difference of birth-rates is not compensated by an equal difference in their death-rates), that population will undergo a change of quality; and a small difference of birth-rate is capable of producing a surprisingly large change of quality in the course of a few generations. We have overwhelmingly strong grounds for believing that in this country (and in almost all the countries of Western civilization) the birth-rate of the inferior half of the population is very considerably greater than that of the superior half; and this greater birth-rate is only very partially compensated by a higher death-rate. The problem of eugenics is to equalize the birth-rate of the two halves (while all efforts to reduce to a minimum the death-rate of both halves are continued), or, if possible, to reverse the prevailing tendency and to secure, in the superior half of the population, a higher birth-rate than that of the inferior half. If the present state of affairs shall continue, the civilization of America is doomed to rapid decay. If equalization of the birth-rate of the two halves can be brought about, the country may face the future with some hope of continued prosperity. If the present tendency can be reversed, and the birth-rate of the superior half be maintained at a higher rate than that of the inferior half, then, even though the difference be but slight, the American people may face the future with a well-grounded hope that they are building up the greatest nation and the most

glorious civilization that the world has ever seen, a
nation capable of assuming the leadership of the world
and of securing the reign of justice, freedom, and
kindness throughout every land.[1]

The knowledge we have amply justifies the eugenic
demand; the facts are becoming, and will become,
more and more widely appreciated; a strong public
opinion is being created. But given the diffusion of
such knowledge and such public opinion, how shall
they be applied to secure the desired effects? It is
now generally agreed that the reproduction of the
least fit, especially of those persons who are indis-
putably feeble-minded, should be prevented. Public
opinion is already aroused on this matter; some steps
have been taken, and others will follow. There is
good ground for hope that within a few decades all
the United States of America will effectively deal with
this most immediately urgent evil, the high birth-rate
of the admittedly and grossly unfit. It is needless to
argue here the relative advantages of sterilization
and institutional segregation. Probably both methods will be used.

---

[1] I leave out of account in this summary statement the
effects of immigration. Public opinion on that matter is
already strongly aroused; the bearing and importance of
the immigration problem are so obvious that it is incredi-
ble the American people should remain indifferent and
inert in face of it, and should not take very soon the
strictest measures to prevent the immigration of all but
those persons who are in every way well fitted to become
good American citizens in the fullest sense of the words.

But such measures, though they will immediately obviate a large amount of human suffering and will effect a great public economy, will postpone only a little the deterioration of quality which threatens the whole nation with decay. Some writers on this topic (*e. g.*, Professor Knight Dunlap in his "Personal Beauty and Race Betterment") have expressed the hope that the wider diffusion of knowledge of methods of birth-control (the contra-ceptive methods) will have a very beneficial effect. Up to the present, such knowledge, diffusing itself downward through the social strata, seems to have diminished very markedly the reproduction of that part of the population (amounting perhaps nearly to one-half of it) which is above the average (statistically) in native qualities; so that its effects hitherto have been gravely dysgenic or racially detrimental. Further diffusion may partially rectify this dysgenic influence; but it seems highly improbable that it can, of itself, ever completely neutralize it; it is still more improbable that such knowledge will ever operate as a positively eugenic influence.

Professor Dunlap is optimistic enough to suppose that the further diffusion of this knowledge will solve the "Negro problem" of America. It is to be feared that it will have, among the colored people, only the positively dysgenic effects which it already produces on so great a scale in the white population; that among both white and colored people it will be put into practice only by the more far-sighted, prudent, and self-controlled; while the most ignorant, careless, and improvident will continue to behave as they always have behaved.

Something may be hoped from the influence upon individual conduct of an enlightened public opinion and sentiment. But, again, it seems highly improbable that this factor alone, or in conjunction with the one last considered, will ever suffice to reverse or even to arrest the process of deterioration.[1] There can be little doubt that the economic factor is of dominant importance in determining the rate of reproduction in all classes but the very poorest and the very richest. The outstanding fact of our present civilization is that the vast majority of men and women are striving to rise, or to maintain themselves, in the social and economic scale, and that the addition of each child to a family is a very serious handicap, a great additional weight, to be borne by the parents who are engaged in this struggle. The acute realization of this fact is the principal ground of the restriction of the birthrate in recent times among those who have succeeded in rising above the lower social levels. If this be admitted, and I do not think it is seriously questioned by any one who is competent to form an opinion in the matter, it follows that we must look to some readjustment of family incomes as the chief eugenic measure of the future. It may be remarked that no general raising of the level of prosperity and of the standard of living is likely to have the desired effect in any appreciable degree. For the demands

---

[1] It is notorious that the crusade of President Roosevelt and of many other eminent men against "race suicide" seems to have made no appreciable effect.

of men (and of women) for the good things which money can secure are practically unlimited; and the demands or desires for such things of any particular family are, in the main, relative to the standard set by their social equals, by the social circle to which by occupation and education they belong. This standard of demand at any social level is the product of the interplay of many factors, and, though it undergoes absolute and relative changes, it is fairly stable. In the main it corresponds to the purchasing power of the remuneration commonly received by persons of the average education and abilities of the class concerned; and this remuneration tends in the main to be such as will permit the satisfaction of the standard demands of a family of three or four persons, that is, a family containing one or two children. Each addition to the family, beyond this minimum number, entails an inability to attain the satisfaction of the standard demands of the class to which it belongs, entails the going without some one or more of the good things of life which other families of similar social level enjoy—it may be domestic help, a piano, an automobile, college education for the children, foreign travel, a country house, etc., etc. Nor would an absolute equality of income for all families and classes meet the case. If that state of affairs could be maintained, it is clear, I think, that its effects would be positively dysgenic in a high degree. It is equally clear that the general indiscriminating State endowment of motherhood, now called for in so many quarters, would have directly dysgenic effects; and it would be disastrous, in that it would go very far to destroy the family as an institution of any nation which should adopt this plan. All such schemes should be condemned on the general and sufficient ground that the national welfare and social justice demand that each worker should be remunerated in proportion to the value of the services that he renders to the community. For only in this way are men effectively stimulated to put forth their best efforts, and to prepare themselves and their children to render the more valuable and more arduous and (what is in the main the same thing) the more intellectual forms of service.

What is required to counteract the very powerful dysgenic influence of the economic consideration, or prudence, is that every family which has risen above the mean social level (or, better still perhaps, every family which has any good claim to belong to what may be called "the selected classes") should know that the addition of each child should automatically bring with it an increase of income sufficient to meet the expenses normally incurred in the bringing up of that child. It is clear that, in order to meet this requirement, the amount of increase of income would have to bear some given proportion to the income already enjoyed or earned. This increase of income should, I suggest, be not less than one-tenth of the earned income, and might well be rather more. A family earning an income of $2,000 a year would then receive, for each living child under the age of say twenty years, an additional income of $200 a year. If such increase of income, proportional to the earnings and to the number of children, could be secured to each family of the selected classes, the eugenic effect would, I submit, be very great, far surpassing in this direction the effect of any other eugenic measure that has been proposed; while it would do nothing to diminish the natural and proper incentives to effort, and would not in any way tend to diminish the sense of parental responsibility or to weaken family ties.

The question arises, then—Is there any way in which we may hope to see such an adjustment of incomes brought about? In a paper published many years ago,[1] I suggested that the State and the municipalities, which employ a large and constantly increasing number of selected servants, should introduce remuneration on this plan into all their services. I urged that, if this were done, public opinion would be quick to recognize the essential justice, as well as the social and eugenic expediency, of the plan, and would bring such pressure to bear on all large employers of skilled labor, that they might be led to follow suit. It is interesting to note that, since my suggestion was made, some small steps have been made in this direction; though it is clear that these steps were due to recognition of their essential justice, rather than to consideration of their eugenic effects; for statesmen remain

[1] "A Practicable Eugenic Suggestion," a paper read before the British Sociological Society and published in *Sociological Papers*, vol. II, London, 1909.

absolutely blind and ignorant in face of the eugenic problem. I refer more especially (1) to the small remissions of income tax made by the British Government on account of children of persons of small incomes; (2) to the separation allowances paid to soldiers by the British and other governments during the war. In the British army these allowances were made larger in proportion to the number of children and in proportion to the rank and pay of the soldier; so that a sergeant-major, for example, with a large family received a very much larger pay than an unmarried private. This was essentially just, and was generally approved; and it was also eugenic. But that the eugenic consideration played no part in determining this scale seems clear from the fact that (until near the end of the war, when some slight change was made) the plan was not applied to the commissioned officers. The British Government thus let slip an opportunity to put in practice a eugenic measure of tremendous power, which would have been universally welcomed and approved, and which would have done something to compensate for the terrible losses of human qualities which the country suffered in the war. For there, in the commissioned ranks, were practically all the most capable and healthy young men of the British Empire, all the most desirable fathers, selected from all the manhood of the Empire by the stringent tests of achievement in the field and success in the officers' training-schools. The ignorance and folly of a government which let pass this opportunity, while recognizing in its treatment of the non-commissioned ranks the essential justice of this plan of remuneration, is deplorable, both on account of the grave injustice done to so many brave men and on account of the many fine children they might have fathered under the plan, but who were never conceived.[1] Yet, in spite of the loss of this great opportunity and of the official ignoring of the eugenic effects of remuneration on the new plan, the fact that it was applied throughout the non-commissioned ranks is very encouraging; for it constituted official recognition of the justice of this plan and familiarized the public with the principle.

I can see no reason why, in this and in every civilized country, this new plan of remuneration should not be applied forthwith to every State and municipal service, with great eugenic effects. But I recognize difficulties in the way of supposing that the same plan might be universally or widely adopted by private firms or by public and semi-public corporations and institutions not supported by taxation. Let us consider the case of the teachers in those educational institutions which are not wholly supported by public funds. To make the problem more concrete, let us take the case of the teachers in an endowed university, such as Harvard or Yale, institutions which, next to the States and the municipalities, might be expected to be most readily moved by enlightened regard for

---

[1] There were non-commissioned officers with families who refused to accept commissions because they could not afford to do so.

eugenic principles. The president has at his disposal a certain amount of income for payment of salaries. He rightly desires to include in the faculty the largest possible number of men of high ability and achievement. Two candidates for a post appear to be equally well qualified; but one of them is a bachelor, or has a small family; the other, though of the same age, already has a large family. Which will the president appoint, if the "new plan" has been adopted? Similar difficulties in the working of the plan would arise in—and would be even more serious in—any corporation whose primary aim was the making of profits. It is perhaps hardly to be hoped that—even if the "new plan" were enforced by legislation in the public services, the army, the navy, the civil service, the municipal services, and so forth—example and the force of public opinion could secure its effective adoption in the remuneration of all selected classes of workers. What possibilities of its general adoption remain? I can think of two only, or rather two varieties of one scheme; namely, the setting apart of a national fund for the supplementing of salaries of selected workers according to the "new plan." This national fund might be provided by taxation; or it might be created, and increased from time to time, by the public spirit and beneficence of rich men. We have already seen the late Andrew Carnegie provide a pensions fund for selected university professors. May we not hope for the realization of this more far-reaching scheme, which, from the points of view of both social justice and national welfare, would be so admirable. I can think of no other purpose to which the rich man who wishes to promote the welfare of his kind, both in the present and for all time, could so confidently devote his wealth, without risk of pauperizing any individual, or of doing any social injury that might offset the benefits he aimed to confer on his fellow men. In order to make the "new plan" as wide in its operation as is desirable, a very large sum would be required; but in the first instance it might be applied to some one highly selected class, such as the teachers in colleges and universities. For not only are such teachers in the main a very highly selected class, embodying much of the best human qualities of the whole country; they are also notoriously a class which is restricted in reproduction by the narrowness of its means; and they are a class whose remuneration is in the hands of responsible governing bodies, which might be trusted to administer with discretion and fairness any moneys derived from "the national fund for the new plan."

In view of the difficulty of moving legislatures to action directed to the good of posterity, it seems probable that the best hope of instituting the new plan lies in the possibility of raising the required national fund by appeal to private beneficence. It might be hoped that, if in this way a beginning were once made, the State legislatures or, better still, the federal government, might later be led to appreciate the value of the new plan, to adopt it in the payment of all public servants, and to create the large national fund necessary for its general application on the widest possible scale.

If the new plan were adopted in Great Britain, it might save some remnants of the old professional class which, the product of a long process of selection, has been the repository of a very large proportion of the best qualities of the British stock and the source of most of the leaders in all departments of the national life. This class, on which the burdens of the war fell more heavily than on any other, is now being rapidly taxed out of existence.

APPENDIX IV

Registration of Family Histories

Although I regard the "new plan" sketched in
Appendix III as the most important eugenic measure
that can be advocated with any hope of success, I
recognize that we cannot afford to neglect any other
measure of eugenic tendency; and I propose here
another such reform which, as public opinion becomes
enlightened, might be of great value, and might be
put into operation without great cost and without any
interference with the liberty of the individual. I suggest that every State should institute a voluntary
registration of family histories, and should keep, in
clear and easily consulted form, a record of all family
histories thus registered.

It is one of the gravest evils of the present time,
and a source of terrible hardship to many persons,
that, in choosing a wife or husband, the choice has so
often to be made in almost complete ignorance of
important facts in the family history of the individual
concerned. Many a man (and woman) has found
himself united to a partner whose family history
betrays a strong tendency to insanity, tuberculosis,
or alcohol, or some other grave defect.

If such voluntary registration were instituted, ana
if the State made every effort, by the aid of properly
equipped officials, to verify and check the accuracy of

the recorded information, it would, I think, soon become the custom, for all or most of the more educated part of the community, to register each child in its proper place in the genealogical tables, and to consult these tables (at a small fee, perhaps) when engagement or marriage was contemplated. Even if the young people concerned were slow, in many cases, to take advantage of the information thus rendered available, their parents might be trusted to pay more attention to it, and, in the light of it, to give wise advice, which, when so well founded, would not fail to carry weight. When the system had been in operation for some little time, the mere absence of any family record in the official tables would afford a strong presumption of the existence of some grave defect in the family concerned, and would be a ground for caution and further inquiry. That very many persons are not averse from such recording of their family histories, and even their publication at large, is shown by the columns devoted to genealogies of citizens in some of the leading newspapers of America.

Some of the most prominent advocates of eugenic measures have been bachelors or childless men, and in some cases they have been persons whose family relations have in other ways departed from the normal and generally desirable type. It thus happens that the eugenists have been laid open to the retort—Why don't you practise what you preach? In order to defend myself in advance from any such reproach, I publish a little picture of my children as they appeared in the year 1914. I indulge at the same time a form of pride of which no man need feel ashamed. In the pages of this book I may seem to have said some hard things about the Amer can nation. Let me here point out that, in bringing my children to dwell in this country, I have paid to its people the highest and sincerest compliment that any man could offer.

APPENDIX VI

I add a short list of the books which seem to me best suited to give the general reader further information concerning the main topic discussed in the foregoing pages:

"Applied Eugenics," by Paul Popenoe (editor of the *Journal of Heredity*) and R. H. Johnson. New York: The Macmillan Co., 1918.

This is, I think, the best general discussion of eugenic problems and principles for the general reader.

"The Racial Prospect," by S. K. Humphrey. New York: Charles Scribner's Sons, 1920, and "Mankind," by the same author and publisher, 1917.

These two books are excellent discussions of human qualities, with special reference to the future in America.

"The Old World in the New," by E. A. Ross (Professor of Sociology in the University of Wisconsin). New York: The Century Co., 1914.

A discussion of "The Significance of Past and Present Immigration to the American People." The author cites many facts of observation and many weighty opinions which illustrate the reality of racial peculiarities and their persistence and influence under changed environment. The careful reader will see that these, in the main, agree closely with the evidence and findings of my pages; compare, *e. g.*, what is said on pages 113 *et seq.* on the low level of intelligence and the character traits of the immigrants from Southern Italy. It is much to be desired that every American citizen should read this book with an open mind. Says this high authority: "Not until the twenty-first century will the philosophic historian be able to declare with scientific certitude that the cause of the mysterious decline that came upon the American people early in the twentieth century was the deterioration of popular intelligence by the admission of great numbers of backward immigrants."

"The Direction of Human Evolution," by E. G. Conklin (Professor of Biology in Princeton University). New York: Charles Scribner's Sons, 1921.

An excellent popular discussion of human and racial qualities from the eugenic and political point of view by a distinguished biologist.

"Population and Birth Control," edited by E. and C. Paul. New York: The Critic and Guide Company, 1917.

Written by a dozen writers of widely dissimilar views, this book contains a very thorough and well-balanced discussion of that all-important topic, birth control, its eugenic and dysgenic tendencies and possibilities.

"The Revolutions of Civilization," by Professor Flinders Petrie. New York: Harper Bros., 1919.

An impressive picture of the rise and fall of civilizations by this eminent archæologist and Egyptologist.

This is only a small selection from a large and rapidly increasing literature. I wish to point out to readers that they are not to regard this selection as one-sided and biassed. The most striking fact about the present situation is that, while popular and journalistic opinion refuses in the main to face the racial problem and to take seriously the propaganda of the eugenists, all the facts, all authority, and all instructed and weighty opinion converge to show the supreme importance of this problem and of this propaganda.

INDEX

French, the, qualities of, 105, 111; components of, 109; and British, 145
Freud, S., 127, 129

Galton, F., 59
Garnett, Maxwell, 69
Garth, R., 56
Gehring, A., 73, 77
Genius, 40
German docility, 113
Gobineau, Count, 25
Goddard, H. H., 43, 166
Grant, Madison, 28
Great Britain, 157
Great War and knowledge, 3
Greece, 168
Gregarious instinct, 82

Halford, S. H., 150, 156
Harvard graduates, 164
Heron, D., 188
Hertz, F., 27
Hindus, 68
Hirsch, N. D., 44
Homicide, 97
Human reservoirs, 3
Humphrey, S. K., 211
Hunter, R., 56
Huot, 119

Idiots, 40
Illiterates, 45
Immigration, 160, 195
Impairment of qualities, 16
Inadequacy of qualities, 12
Inbreeding, 10
Indians, 56
Instincts of man, 76
Intellectual energy, 51
Intellectual forms, 137
Intelligence, inborn, 47, 52, 59
Intelligence of children, 50, 57, 61, 65
Intelligence and morals, 135

Intelligence and social status, 63
Intercourse of peoples, 14
Introverts, 85
Iseman, M. S., 160
Italians, 64, 65

James, William, 69, 76
Jews, 28, 33, 127
Johnson, R. H., 189, 211
Jung, C. G., 85, 124

Knowledge, effects of new, 2; and wisdom, 11
Kornhauser, A. W., 152

Langfeld, H. S., 73
Leisure, 13
Literates and illiterates, 45

Manual workers, 185
Medical profession, the, 166
Mental defect hereditary, 42
Mental defectives, 40, 165
Mental tests, 43
Mesopotamia, 8
Mill, J. S., 20
Moral chaos, 15
Moral qualities, 67, 135
Moral sentiments, 130
Morals, and art, 72; and intelligence, 135
Morselli, E., 92, 96
Muddle, British, 112, 116
Mulatto intelligence, 55
Musical talent, 124
Mutiny, Indian, 71

National character, 33
National fund, 204
National institutions, 146
Negro, the, intelligence of, 54, 57; moral qualities of, 117
Neo-Darwinism, 128
Nervous troubles, 87

Anti-Movements in America

An Arno Press Collection

Ku Klux Klan. **Papers Read at the Meeting of Grand Dragons Knights at Their First Annual Meeting.** [1923]

McCarthy, Joseph. **McCarthyism:** The Fight for America. 1952

McDougall, William. **Is America Safe for Democracy?** 1921

Monk, Maria. **Awful Disclosures.** 1836

[Morse, Samuel Finley Breese]. **Foreign Conspiracy Against the Liberties of the United States.** 1835

National Americanism Commission of the American Legion, Compiler. **ISMS:** A Review of Alien Isms, Revolutionary Communism and Their Active Sympathizers in the United States. 1937

Nevins, William. **Thoughts on Popery.** 1836

Pope, Or President? Startling Disclosures of Romanism as Revealed by Its Own Writers. 1859

[Priest, Josiah]. **Slavery.** 1843

Reed, Rebecca Theresa. **Six Months in a Convent and Supplement.** 1835

Roberts, Kenneth L. **Why Europe Leaves Home.** 1922

Ross, Edward Alsworth. **Standing Room Only?** 1927

Schaack, Michael J. **Anarchy and Anarchists.** 1889

Schultz, Alfred P. **Race or Mongrel.** 1908

Stripling, Robert E. **The Red Plot Against America.** 1949

Tenney, Jack B. **Red Fascism.** 1947

[Timayenis, Telemachus T.] **The Original Mr. Jacobs:** A Startling Exposé. 1888

Wiggam, Albert Edward. **The Fruit of the Family Tree.** 1924

Anti-Catholicism in America, 1841-1851: Three Sermons. 1977

Anti-Semitism in America, 1878-1939. 1977